SUCCEEDING AT BUSINESS IN SOUTHEAST ASIA

SUCCEEDING AT BUSINESS IN SOUTHEAST ASIA

Common Mistakes Companies Make and How to Avoid Them

Eric Moraczewski

 The Association of
Accountants and
Financial Professionals
in Business

ISBN Print: 978-0-996-72936-9
ISBN ePDF: 978-1-119-73706-3
ISBN ePUB: 978-1-119-73705-6

V10018782_052620

A special thanks to my wife, Kathryn, who sticks with me and supports me no matter how busy I get, and to my children, James and Nora, whom Kathryn and I are so very fortunate to have in our lives. Thank you also to my parents, sister, and my in-laws who help us so much as we take on work, school, and everything else that comes up in our lives.

Contents

Contents

Introduction

Over the course of the last 10 years I have been involved in doing business on four continents, in 20+ countries, and more cities than I can count. My experience has led me to appreciate a lot, understand some, and teach a little bit. I have presented at conferences and seminars, primarily on Asia, and specifically on China, regarding private equity, how Chinese capital is affecting business in the United States, business opportunities in Asia, and human resource practices in Asia. Currently, I run a cross-border growth strategy company called FDI Strategies where we build market entry strategy, put together a plan, and help a company execute these strategies. Truly, it is a lot of fun working with companies from assorted industries, with varying needs and distinctly different opportunities. No two days are alike and every day is exciting. More than anything, I am blessed to work with special people every day of my life, from our board of directors to our interns. This enthusiastic, exceptional team makes me look better than I am and ensures that every day is rewarding.

My background is in finance and accounting; needless to say, I like numbers. When I think about some of our clients who focus solely on the United States, I am mindful of the fact that the United States makes up five percent of the world economy (based upon population). This is a large number for one country, no doubt, but it also shows that there's immense potential outside of the U.S market. If only there was an extremely large population somewhere in the world with a growing middle class who was beginning to consume more and more. Oh wait, there is—Southeast Asia! Today, Asia makes up roughly 60 percent of the world economy based on population. The Southeast Asian markets have seen immense growth over the last 20 years and continue to evolve every day; perhaps most compelling is the speed at which this demographic is increasing. No longer does it take 50 years for a middle class to evolve. In the last 10 years, while traveling back and forth from China, I have witnessed dramatic change.

My goal in this book is to walk you through the steps necessary to build and execute a market entry strategy into Southeast Asia, similar to what we do with our clients at FDI Strategies. You will learn about the top five pitfalls as well as common areas of concern and mistakes, in a step-by-step manner. These can be internal or external issues, they can be country-specific or endemic to the region, but they all are issues we have regularly seen with clients and other businesses. I have tried, where possible, to use examples—concrete illustrations—based on my own career experience to help reveal the bigger picture and affirm that you are not the only one who makes mistakes. As I've learned from hard experience, mistakes are also great opportunities for personal growth and knowledge.

My primary focus is on showing you how to develop a strategy, use that strategy to build a plan, and use that plan to execute and succeed in the market. After all, we all want to succeed. Putting our best foot forward is the first step toward finding success.

I will also examine topics that may apply to some, but not all, companies—joint ventures, franchising strategy, and how small businesses might go about developing their own Asian market entry strategy. In addition, I will also touch on the relationships that most people already have and do not know they have, and how to utilize those relationships. Finally, I will explore the takeaways from your Asian strategy and operations. This is important because, while it is great to grow your business in a foreign country, there are many lessons you can learn from foreign operations and apply to your home market.

If you do not do this, you are not maximizing the value that can be derived from your international expansion.

Developing a strategy involves examining several things. To begin with, we look at a firm's history to understand why a company is where it is currently and to gain an understanding of what brought it to that point, which provides an overall understanding of the firm. From there, we look at the external environment, the factors that exert a force on the firm and then the forces the firm exerts on the external environment. Many times we forget about how much the external environment propels a company in a certain direction, but laws change and companies shift. Consider the Affordable Care Act in the United States: it would be hard to find a company that this legislation did not affect. Finally, we look at the present environment, what is going on within the firm and what effect these internal dynamics may have on the business as a whole.

This process tells us where a firm is today, how it got there, and what forces are playing on it. We use the same process if we are looking at expansion into foreign countries or looking to help a company build an overall strategy within its current markets. If you do not understand where your company is and where it has come from, how can you ever expect to know where it is headed?

FDI's director of strategy spent many years in the Air Force as a chief strategist and taught strategy to the Air Force leadership. He likens much of strategy to a ship in the ocean: think Christopher Columbus sailing to the New World and the currents that pushed him toward his destination (and out of Spain). These currents are his history and his present, but they also affect where he will go in the future.

Once you've assessed where you came from, you must figure out where you are going. When referring specifically to Southeast Asia, you need to look at who you are as a company and how you can map your strengths to what you are looking to do in those markets. So, if you are selling a new technology that needs a very established infrastructure, you should probably look at the opportunities of Japan, perhaps Singapore, or even Korea; you should probably not look to Malaysia, Myanmar, or Indonesia. Using what you know about your company and your abilities, as well as your interests in the markets, you can select a country, or, perhaps, if you have the resources, several countries.

Once you have decided on your focus market, how are you going to enter this market? Do you need a partner to enter the market? Are you setting up a Wholly Owned Foreign Entity (WOFE) or forming a joint venture or even franchising your business? Do you need to set up a holding company in a foreign market first? In some instances this is still necessary in China, it is still necessary for work in North Korea, and it can be helpful in several other countries. Will you manufacture in the market itself, or import all goods from your home market? Will manufacturing in the market help develop sales opportunities? How do you develop distributor relationships?

Many of these questions will be answered by a consulting team or an in-country manager that you hire. It is important to hire an in-country manager and have some boots on the ground. Without an active presence on the ground, you are typically setting yourself up for failure. But it goes beyond just having an active presence. Are you giving that person/those people the resources they need to succeed? If you're not giving them the resources to succeed, you cannot expect success.

Next, it's time to execute. The previous steps comprise the strategy and planning phase; both are very important, but without execution, those two steps do not mean much. With great execution but no strategy and planning, some businesses nevertheless achieve minimal success. A good company is often good at execution and planning, but if they're good at developing and evolving their strategy as well, they're often a very successful business.

So assuming you have your markets and plans in place, putting in continuous checks and balances allows you to make adjustments to your execution. This will ensure you do not stray too far in the wrong direction, or, better still, these continuous checks mean you are maximizing your opportunities and capturing the most market share possible. Properly calibrated, the balance you achieve allows for fluid movement so that your business has enough opportunities to succeed. Most people believe that with a good plan and a leader in place, things should just work out, and we hope they do, but plans need to be retooled with time and education so that you adhere to the lines of your overall strategy.

Think again of Christopher Columbus. Imagine him steering the Niña, the Pinta, and the Santa María across the Atlantic through currents and wind streams. What if he saw a storm in the distance—wouldn't he look to avoid it, if possible, by shifting course? But if shifting course would not avoid the storm or would move him into a worse part of the storm, no doubt Columbus would have sealed the ships up and protected what he could hoping to get through with as little damage as possible. The same is true of your business. In any market, you will come across issues, and you'll need to decide whether or not you will forge ahead and move forward into the storm or avoid that path if possible.

Now you have a general idea of our process. In this book, our focus will be on how to do this in relation to Southeast Asia. Full disclosure: A large part of my work in Southeast Asia has been in China. Recently, as I was contemplating the last 10 years of my life during which I lived in Washington, D.C, and Colorado Springs, Colo., it occurred to me that roughly one full year of those 10 years of my life was spent in Asia, roughly 10 percent of my time; and probably 90 percent of that time was spent in China. Obviously, there were times I was there more than others, but it adds up very quickly.

I mention this to give you an idea of the dedication required to build operations in Asia. Do not think that you will be able to fly in and fly out every once in a while. If you want to build sustainable operations, you need to show commitment to it, and part of that commitment is leadership time. There are several clients or potential clients in Asia who, every time I see them, want to know when I'll be back; I doubt this is just because they want to see me again. It's a question of commitment—telling them how often I will return and showing them what type of relationship we have the potential to develop if we do business together in the future. There are other commitments, such as in-country operations, which we'll talk about as we go forward. But it's important that you know this is a top-to-bottom commitment and decision.

"Commitment" is an important word when referring to Asia. Of course, it's important in all markets, but commitment takes on many different meanings in Asia. There is the time and capital commitment that many think of initially. There's a commitment to your partners, as you show them *how* you will work together, and that you are someone they want to work with in the future. There's a commitment to that country's government that you often make by devising a long-term business plan; a surprise to many from the United States or Europe is how often this is requested when you set up operations. Finally, there's a commitment to your customers or clients, assuring them that you will not leave tomorrow and that your products and services will be supported in the future.

My background and personal experience in Asia is reflected in stories I recount throughout the book to provide color and offer a better understanding of specific areas that may cause problems. So, to begin, my initial foray into Asia began roughly a decade ago, while working for Gallagher & Associates, a museum planning and design firm. The company was setting up operations in Asia by forming a joint venture in Singapore. This was an easy entry into the Asian markets; I often refer to Singapore as "Asia-lite." Singapore provides a great jumping off point in a beautiful location (think of Hawaii and New York City blended—this is Singapore), but also a very friendly country in which to work abroad. It was easier for Gallagher & Associates because we formed a joint venture with a company that we had worked with since 1979 (yes, relationships matter above all else in Asia). Over the next couple of years, we grew operations in Singapore and started taking on projects throughout Asia.

Eventually, the company was hired to design the Shanghai Natural History Museum, a project that required our physical presence in China. It was then that I began commuting back and forth to set up our offices, registering us as a Wholly Owned Foreign Enterprise (WOFE), and establishing relationships with lawyers, accountants, banks, and other service providers. As our business grew over the next several years, I continued commuting. After being present from the project's inception, witnessing all that went into building the museum along with our company's sustained presence in China, the day the Shanghai Natural History Museum opened was really exciting.

Roughly three years ago, after spending the last seven years working in various international markets and at the request of several investors, I started my own business in Colorado Springs. The business, FDI Strategies, is focused on foreign direct investment into and outside of the U.S. market. Because the large part of my experience was in Asia, we initially focused on Asia, with much of that focus on China. During this time, I traveled to Hong Kong, Taiwan, and Japan, and incorporated meetings with companies from Vietnam, Malaysia, India, and many other countries. We were fortunate enough to work with companies both in the United States and abroad in a wide range of sectors, including construction, data storage, medical devices, food and beverage, consumer goods, and more. During the last three years, there has rarely been a day that I have not learned something new, either about countries, regions, or industries.

In 2015, I was fortunate to be invited to join the Governor of Colorado's Trade Delegation traveling to Japan and China. Because of my experience in China, I planned that portion of the group's itinerary. This trip opened my eyes to a different side of doing business in Asia. Because I was traveling with Governor John Hickenlooper, doors opened quickly—much more quickly than when I was traveling on my own on business. It also changed previously established relationships.

> ➤ *The takeaway:* Get to know people, develop relationships, and it will help you continue to grow your company, especially in relationship-driven cultures across Asia, where relationships are fundamental to success.

It's important to note that while there are many practices in Asia that we are not accustomed to in the United States, there are also some fundamental similarities to which we all can relate. When a Chinese company is setting up operations in the United States and sending over an executive to run the new operation, they want two specific things: *First,* they want great food (specifically, great food they are used to), and second, they want better for their children than they have, or had, for themselves. These two pieces of information are critical because, at the end of the day, no matter what the culture, we strive for many of the same things. I often tell people that when I travel abroad I love the food I get to try, but eventually, come day six or seven of my trip, I just want a cheeseburger and fries. Take this further and think about moving abroad: Eventually you will want your own comfort food; the same holds true for someone coming to either the United States or Europe from Asia.

The second similarity is perhaps even more fundamental than food, and that is the desire to protect, provide, and improve the lives of our families. My parents and my in-laws worked extremely hard throughout their lives to make sure that their children were not only able to get a walking start in life but hit the ground running. One of the most important lessons I learned in life is that there are two things that lead to success—hard work and intelligence—and you can control only one of those. This is something I learned from my father, not through his words but by his actions. Now, as a father, I want to be able to provide even more for my children. Many Asians have this same mentality, and this is why you see their children coming to study in the United States and Europe, why you see parents driving their children to do and be more.

It is important to remember to pay attention to the differences in cultures between the United States and Europe and Asia. Not recognizing them can be the difference between success and failure. But it is our similarities that bring us together, and in a relationship-driven culture, building on those similarities can result in a tightly bound friendship. It can be what differentiates you from your competition.

CHAPTER 1

The Importance of Relationships: How to Build and Maintain Them

A relationship-based sales approach will maximize the future value of an opportunity. A transactional-based sales approach will maximize only today's value.

Asian culture is a culture based upon relationships. These relationships mean more to Asian businesspeople than any other business skill set. Their premise is that if I can trust the person I am working with, together we can figure out how to do something. It also has a lot to do with "saving face" in a business environment. If you are responsible for hiring someone and six months later they get caught stealing from the company, this reflects as poorly on you as it does on the person actually stealing. Why should someone trust your judgment in the future if you were willing to bring this person into the business? Similarly, if this is a person you would associate with, are you the person I should associate with my business? The other focus here is that a relationship is not short-term; it is a long-term view that says we will work together for years and years to come. Oftentimes during this process, personal and professional relationships intersect.

I recently took on a client for U.S. expansion after becoming acquainted with the spouse of one of the company's vice presidents years ago. Any time I am in China, I get together with this person because he has become a friend. We have explored some business opportunities together but never done business together. When his wife's company had a need, I was the first, and only, person they called for their growth. This is actually a common phenomenon that I did not foresee years ago when our friendship first began.

The Critical Importance of Face Time

Far too often we see people in the United States trying to form or build a relationship, meaning they either reach out directly, or they try to build relationships through social media websites like WeChat and Weibo; some have also started to utilize U.S. websites like LinkedIn. This type of relationship building may work well in the United States and yield results eventually, but this is not the best way to build relationships with Asian businesses.

A problem that often arises is that agreements need to be signed by high-ranking officials in the company, senior leadership, who are not always in the market and available to sign agreements. Figuring out a way to manage this is critical. Among the factors to be considered are the size and value of a client, the potential of the client, and what other opportunities await beyond the signing ceremony. If the potential across all of these factors is low, a company may choose to have a local market leader sign the document. If it is big enough, it may be a country or regional leader, and if it is really big, someone from headquarters may come over to sign the agreement. Reading the appropriate nature of the ceremony is key to knowing who should attend it.

There are various ways to build relationships in Asia. A few of the better ones are:

- **Meet people face-to-face using your current network**. Having someone introduce and vouch for you allows the person you are trying to build a relationship with not to question your value.

- **Attend trade shows and conferences**. While this seems very similar to a blind email, it tends to yield better results. By attending conferences where key prospective clients are present, you maximize your opportunities. A better way to go about this, if possible, is to speak at conferences in Asia attended by key prospective clients. Letting the conference "vouch" for your capability is a great way to enhance your status.

- **Travel with a trade delegation**. This can also be a great way to build new relationships—if the delegation is going to meet with the "right" people—otherwise you may find yourself making relationships that are not useful to you. The United States-Vietnam Chamber of Commerce regularly travels to Vietnam as part of a delegation. When doing so, high-ranking officials from Vietnam show up to meet the trade delegation and encourage business through tax incentives, location incentives, and other opportunities that might not be readily identifiable from abroad. There are similar organizations for almost every country, and they each have unique contacts that can be very beneficial to your country.

➤ *The takeaway:* None of these efforts are done from your office or home. If you are building a relationship without meeting the person, 99 percent of the time, it will fall apart or, worse yet, there will be more negative aspects to the relationship than positives where you waste time, energy, and money and have no chance of success.

Understand the Power Structure

In Asia, more often than not, there is only one decision maker at a company, usually the CEO, president, or chairman of the board, but occasionally that's not the case. Pay attention to subtle cues in a meeting, such as seating placement, who walks into the room first and last, and how your counterparts interact with each other. Usually who can and will make the decisions in a meeting is obvious, but not always.

In addition, make sure that you appropriately recognize the importance of people in the meeting. For example, it is customary to bring a small gift to present to your counterparts; make sure the nicest gift goes to the most important person and so on down the line. Some of this has been eliminated in Asian governments as anticorruption practices move forward, but giving a nice sample of your product, a gift from your home state or country (in Colorado, an aspen leaf is a very common and pretty gift, and several fit in your luggage—a flight consideration), or something that you know might be important to the person (a French wine might work for someone who studied in France) is still acceptable. The cost of these gifts should be minimal, but they should definitely follow Asian custom. The price of a gift is not the point; it is saying thank you for welcoming you into the meeting. Likewise, your hosts may present you with a gift, like a branded bookmark or a book about the firm's history.

- *The takeaway:* Do not pressure the relationship. Pushing for a close will not go well in Asia. Ironic, isn't it? Since when you walk through the underground markets of China, you're always relentlessly pressured to buy something.

Five Ways to Build Relationships in Southeast Asia

The importance of relationships is addressed in this first chapter because I find it to be the single most significant factor for success in Asia. Relationships tie into many facets of Asian culture, including trust (or lack thereof), quality, and future potential. If you build a strong relationship, there is huge future potential for you to work together for many years to come. I have often seen failure when someone has gone in and tried to dictate terms and conditions to their Asian partner; even a superior product or service cannot save them with this approach.

1. *Spend Time in Southeast Asia*
There is no other way to grow your relationships in Southeast Asia than spending time there. Meet people while you are there, take time to build a relationship, and focus on the people. But, do not just "go there"; go there and use your connections to help you schedule meetings, network your way through society with introductions.

The first time I went to China, I knew three people. Those three people helped me build a network that is active today, and every time I go there, my goal is to look for new connections. I started in China with two very simple questions: Who should I use as an accountant and who should I use as a lawyer? I worked with an amazing lawyer who made some introductions, but, ended up firing the accountant three months later. The accountant did not do anything wrong, per se, but he did not have the knowledge and experience necessary to operate on an international platform. I recommend finding lawyers and accountants that have clients who may be useful to you. After all, there is a mutual benefit. If your business grows, so does the business of your lawyer and accountant, as well as their other clients' businesses. I also recommend you push your lawyers and accountants to create introductions for you, whether it is to their clients or friends.

The other contact in the region that I have learned to use is the U.S. government. U.S. Commercial Services has on-the-ground operations in almost every country in the world, and in certain countries, like Japan, China, and India, they have operations in more than one city. For a small fee ($300–1,000), you will gain introductions, market research, and keen insights into the market that you might not otherwise have had, all of which is not only good not only for making new connections but also good for making sure your strategy and planning align. The other benefit is that in Asia, a government introduction elevates your perceived value in the country. While we in the United States may not place a high value on working with the government unless we are selling to them, that is not true in Asia, so maximizing this opportunity is very important.

Finally, use your other relationships, including friends and consultants. Most expatriates in Asia are extremely open to getting together and talking to someone from home. These people are great resources because they have spent years on the ground developing and building relationships. At FDI Strategies, we encourage our clients to push us, as consultants, for introductions. We regularly make introductions for our clients to potential suppliers, potential clients, and the media. It is a vital part of our business. Despite this, sometimes we overlook someone whom we should introduce a client to; for this reason, our clients are encouraged to continually ask and push us. Explaining why one individual is not a good fit for your client sometimes reminds you that you forgot someone who is a good fit. You never know until you ask; so I encourage you to ask and keep asking. Fortunately, there are many ways to keep up, either through applications like LinkedIn (becoming more and more popular in Asia), through your website, or even through generic requests, such as "Whom should we speak to in the media?" While we don't encourage our clients to make direct requests by going around us, an introduction via email through us can make a world of difference.

2. *Do Not Waste Time*

Most people in the United States or parts of Europe go to Southeast Asia and do not understand the power structure—meaning, who can make decisions in an organization. In India, although officially illegal, caste, where people are born into their roles in life, is the determining factor. This is true in other parts of Asia as well, also in countries like Myanmar and Pakistan, although sometimes it is not seen as clearly as it is in India.

In one meeting, someone mentioned they had never seen an American (me!) do such a good job of not wasting time with people who had no say over anything. My only thought at the time was to get things done, and I knew that to do that, you had to start at the top. If you are just coming into the Southeast Asian market, you have to find a way to navigate and grow your relationships with decision makers and avoid spending time making meaningless connections with executives who cannot advance your cause. You do not always have to follow the traditional path of lower-level introductions. Whether in the United States, China, Japan, or any other country, it is best to take the approach of knowing the people first before trying to sell them something. They are not just potential clients or networking opportunities; they are people with whom you can build an ongoing relationship. In doing so, you will meet some amazing people, try amazing restaurants, and do some business as well. In most of Asia, this is the right way to go about building business. Personally, I do most of the "getting to know" a person outside the office environment—go to lunch or dinner, get to know each other. Even if you are in the office, continue to focus on getting to know the person as a person.

My focus when visiting Asian countries is to work on building my network and relationships. With numerous trips to Asia over the past decade, I have not taken time to visit the many tourist attractions, such as the Great Wall of China. I have been to the Forbidden City, but only for a client meeting. Shanghai has been a frequent destination and I have seen a few more tourist attractions. My point is, do not waste time on yourself; when in Asia, be there to work and make the most of your time.

Also, understand the time involved in getting around in Asia. Taipei is easier to navigate than, say, Hong Kong or Shanghai, but do not think you can set meetings every hour, unless everyone is coming to see you. When you go to Shanghai, Hong Kong, or Beijing, set one appointment in the morning and one appointment in the afternoon, and, perhaps, a dinner (usually in conjunction with an afternoon appointment). My goal is to average between two and two-and-one-half appointments per day on my trips.

3.   *You'll Need Help; Find a Sherpa*
No, not literally a Sherpa, but a guide to navigate you through your city and your contacts. Most people try to do these things on their own and through a few connections; I have done so myself. The beauty of most of the locations you are going to is that someone else has already been there, someone has done it before you, and there are millions of expatriates from the United States and Europe living in Asia. Find the right ones and let them help you navigate the area, either as a paid intermediary or as a new friend in a far-off country.

Among the many other things that you will gain by having your Sherpa help you navigate the society are very interesting stories. More often than not, the Americans I meet in Asia just want to have something in common with someone, so they are happy to try Chinese Chipotle with someone who actually knows what Chipotle is, or to talk about college football to someone familiar with it (they do not need you to talk about NBA basketball in China, or Major League Baseball in Taiwan or Japan, for obvious reasons).

There are many expatriates and locals who are very eager to welcome you and want to get to know you. You can meet people through mutual friends, government introductions, and many other ways such as going to frequented expatriate restaurants and bars or finding expatriate neighborhoods; some you may only meet once or twice, and others you may see almost every time you go to Asia. Similar to meetings in the United States, not everyone you meet is somebody you end up speaking with repeatedly. If you value your relationships very highly, those people will do the same and, in turn, you can build something special.

4. *Make the Relationship Meaningful*
I cannot emphasize this enough: A shallow relationship is not the right way to go about things. Develop meaningful relationships in Asia and the benefits will come. Most times I relate this to a client by asking them if they have a short-term or a long-term strategy for the market. If you have a short-term strategy, where you intend to get in, make a sale or two, and get out, you can get by with shallow relationships—or perhaps, no relationships at all. But if you want to have a long-term future in Asia, develop meaningful relationships.

By spending time in Asia and getting to know people, you will build long-term relationships. My old boss traveled to China for the first time in 1979. After years in and out of Asia, the company formed a joint venture in Singapore, based on a friendship he had developed 30 years earlier. During that time, he became the godfather to his friend's daughter, attended family weddings, and, together, they watched their companies grow. This may be the opposite extreme to the way many approach the Asian markets, but this is an example of the long-term view that we have been discussing.

It is not that difficult to make these relationships meaningful, and more than likely you have some of them here in the United States, but perhaps in the States these relationships are more selective. My father was the vice president of sales for

American Greetings for years. He worked across the country with hundreds of clients, but that did not mean that every client was his best friend (or, for that matter, that they even liked each other); but one of his old clients is a friend we get together with in Austin whenever I visit. My parents have vacationed with others, spending time together even after they retired. This is the sort of relationship that you should seek. Again, not everyone will become that lifelong friend, but some will and others will at least respect that you are invested in your relationship with them.

5.   *Do Not Rely on Contracts*

The United States and Europe are societies built upon legal contracts and agreements. If it is in writing and signed, we can count on it, or there are legal repercussions for those who violate the agreement. Many times people go to Asia, get a contract signed by a middle manager and fly home in triumph, only to find out days, weeks, or months later that their contract is worth nothing. There is no plan on the other side to move forward and, likewise, there is no recourse for a broken contract.

If you are getting a legitimate, signed contract (which is still neither meaningful nor legally binding, rather more symbolic and a general guideline), you will go through a signing ceremony with the patriarch or matriarch (there are more and more female heads in private practice these days in Asia), and your contract will be stamped with the company chop (a chop is a government-issued seal or stamp that becomes the official approval for corporate documents). If you set up an operation in Asia, especially China, your company will receive an official "chop" that will be used at the ceremony.

Keep in mind, in Asia, when contracts are being signed, they are not meant to be held to the letter of the law, but instead to be negotiated throughout the life of the contract. I usually tell my clients that they should expect negotiations to go on through two to three weeks past the receipt of payment. This might be a slight exaggeration but not by much. A contract is put in place to set the relationship guidelines, but everything in it, including price, term, product, quality, etc., is still negotiable after the contract is signed.

This goes back to the need for long-term relationships. The stronger your relationship with your counterparts, the better your ability will be to have a solid working relationship with them.

- *The takeaway:* Build the relationship with your counterpart and your contractual obligations will be taken seriously. If you do not take the relationship seriously, the contract may well be worthless.

I emphasize the importance of relationships to help you understand the confines of the culture. Use this knowledge with the intention of building a better business practice and understanding. Relationships in Asia are your number one priority and should remain that way from start to finish (although assuming you have a long-term outlook, there really is no finish). By building these relationships you will accelerate your business's standing in the Asian culture and gain the ability to grow your business and successfully navigate society.

Those individuals that have taken a relationship-driven approach with peers, clients, suppliers, and the government enjoy continued success. I once had an American tell me that I would never be successful in Asia because he had not been successful in Asia. The pure arrogance of the statement says he did not have the right approach to the market and his own hubris caused his failure. Do not let your own vanity get in the way of your success.

CHAPTER 2

The Role Culture Plays in Determining Economic Value

A very simple phrase comes to mind when thinking about the Asian culture: "You get what you pay for!" That said, it does not mean you will not go through a fierce negotiation on the price.

I have yet to meet an Asian culture that did not negotiate on price. Everything is negotiable. Do not forget this when you are pricing your goods, especially in a business-to-business environment. It is also important to remember this when dealing with suppliers: do not take price at face value, even if it is a good one. A good negotiator is truly respected in the Asian culture; someone who does not negotiate may be seen as a lamb about to be fed to the wolves.

If your focus is on sales price, make sure you build this into your manufacturer's suggested retail price (MSRP) or book price. A client negotiating a discount will feel they got a better deal and perhaps be seen as more valuable inside their own organization. Assuming you have initially priced it correctly, you may see a higher sales price than you might otherwise have expected. That said, do not thoroughly overprice your product or you could hurt your discussions.

Negotiation: Price Is Not the Only Consideration

When Gallagher & Associates first began operations in Singapore, we brought a slightly higher price into the market than what was normal at the time. We were not at U.S. pricing yet, but we were above market average. What we discovered was that although price was still negotiated, Gallagher & Associates was also being forced to provide more services than we were accustomed to doing in the United States. It is obviously very hard to raise your price after you have developed a relationship, and we were not a firm that made its money on additional services like some other architecture, engineering, and construction firms.

From Singapore, Gallagher & Associates moved into China. We learned from our experience in Singapore and came in at even higher pricing in China, pricing that was very similar to our operations in the United States. Again, we saw less of a fight over pricing and more negotiation over the scope of the services being offered and the additional work demanded of us. We believed we could offset the cost of some of the larger scope of the work with in-market labor instead of doing it all on U.S. labor and salaries; to some extent this worked and to some extent it did not. Our error was to mistakenly assume we could get the Chinese up to speed on exhibit design quickly enough to keep pace with the project, which did not happen; instead we ended up using a lot more U.S. labor at a much higher cost.

The other area our clients focused on during negotiations was very short turnarounds, meaning they wanted 500,000-square-foot buildings designed and built within 18 to 24 months, well outside of a normal U.S. timeline. At the time, we thought all that was required was to erect a building as quickly as possible and move on to building the next one. In fact, the reason for this requirement had political ramifications. In China, when political figures leave office and move to a new position or retire, they want to make sure that the project gets done on their watch so that they can take credit for it. Therefore, building it in that timeframe was a major value to our clients.

As you can see there are economic, political, and personal values involved that may differ from those in the United States or Europe. Even when there was no fight over price, negotiations were still taking place. Figuring out the interests that your foreign counterpart will focus on is a very important piece of your own work and potential profitability; this is why economic values play such a large role in strategy and planning.

The other thing I always tell clients to focus on is the "why?" By this I mean, why is something they want an economic value? In the Gallagher example, deadlines were based less on when the building would be completed and they could move on to the next project, and more upon the need to complete the project while a political figure was still in office. Once we understood this, we understood our true timeline.

Determining Economic Value

What economic value is most important? Of course, the answer is price, but how you arrive at the price is almost as important as the price itself. For example:

- Have you compared your competitors'—both local competitors and international—local pricing?

- Do international products receive a higher price than local products, either because of a perceived value or safety concerns? For those that do not remember the story, in 2008, 96 people were arrested in China after it was found that 22 dairy companies sold products tainted with melamine, a chemical that can be fatally toxic to babies. In total, 300,000 babies fell ill and six babies died from kidney stones or other issues.[1] Since 2008, the price of foreign baby formula has dramatically risen. Even more prevalent is the rise in the number of travelers bringing baby formula back to China. Ultimately, the Chinese government restricted what could be brought back, especially from Hong Kong, because so much of it was sold on the black market.

Beyond the Chinese market, many countries in Asia saw a rise in the price of baby formula because of 1) a lack of trust in the Chinese products on the shelves and 2) the abundant purchases the Chinese made when they traveled abroad. This is a great example (albeit, a very sad one) of the impact of one country's circumstances on the rest of Asia, as well as how values can adjust and change very quickly.

Five Common Economic-Value Mistakes Companies Make in Southeast Asia

So often when entering a market, we assign our own values to our counterpart and assume that their interests match our own. Yet, more often than not, this is not true.

1. *Competing on Price*
I cannot tell you how often I talk to someone in the United States or Europe whose sales pitch in the West revolves around higher quality at a lower price. To a Westerner, it is all about the best quality at a good price. The same is true for the Asian

---

[1] http://www.nytimes.com/2011/01/15/world/asia/15briefs-Milk.html?rre f=collection%2Ftimestopic%2FMelamine&action=click&contentCollect ion=timestopics&region=stream&module=stream_unit&version=latest& contentPlacement=6&pgtype=collection&_r=0

consumer; in this way, they are no different. But the Asian consumer assumes that a low price means the product is low quality; what a conundrum for a company that operates on a low-cost basis. We will get to that when we examine the "Five Mistakes," but in the meantime remember that focusing solely on price for your goods or services is a big mistake.

Often, imported products sell at a higher price than the country's local goods. If you are in the United States, compare the pricing of a German luxury car versus a Japanese luxury car. For years, German luxury cars have sold at a true premium, even for the luxury car market whereas luxury Japanese cars are only now starting to truly appreciate in value compared with their competition. Even today, a BMW sells for more than a comparable Lexus. Positioning from day one takes a long time to undo, so if you think you can capture market share on price today and correct for price at a later time, more often than not, you are incorrect. At the very least, your time horizon is probably very far off and it will take longer than you thought to correct your market pricing. I would challenge you to name someone who has done this in a short period of time in your own market.

Going back to the Asian market, I repeat, really focus on what you do well; do not focus on price. Focusing on quality, performance, or simply lack of competition is a great way to grow your business in the Asian markets. The factors that make your product better in your own market will make it better in the new market.

The other issue relating to pricing strategy is to know what your foreign counterpart, be they client, supplier, or joint venture partner, actually cares about. In some cases, it may be margin (more likely in Asia when you are dealing with private companies, but, even then, this is not always the situation). In other cases, it may be schedule, quality, or the desire to show they are working with a top-quality international firm. If the negotiation will not be centered on price, but instead on one or more of these other factors, it is a good time to come in at a higher price than you might otherwise have, because frequently your costs will be significantly higher when running through the project. If you are acutely aware of this ahead of time, you will go in with a stronger hand than many of your competitors, in particular, foreign firms, who do not have this sorted out.

For instance, the managing director of a top law firm in Shanghai that had recently won a very large corporate client's business stated that he had spent six-plus months, including at least 10 trips and countless emails and phone calls, trying to win the client, one that he had randomly met at a conference. Upon winning the client over and winning the business for his firm, the client said, "Do you know you were three times higher in price than the second highest bid?" This did not really surprise my acquaintance; but he did ask, why their services were chosen if his fee was so much higher than the competition. The client said there were several factors. *First*, he felt very comfortable and had a good relationship with the lawyer (the consequence of all the trips, emails, and phone calls). *Second*, the firm had the international prestige the company was looking for, and it was able to provide everything for them that others either could not or did not have the experience to provide. It's a great story and one I wish I could emulate more often, as we would all like to be able to charge three times what our competitors do and still win business. But, it also shows that if you understand the values being brought to the table, your business will be in good shape.

2.   *Closing Instead of Negotiating*
In the United States, we have fallen in love with the *Glengarry Glen Ross* saying, "ABC... Always Be Closing" or perhaps another saying of similar merit, "Coffee is for Closers." In Asia, these sayings change to "ABN... Always Be Negotiating!"

Although you should not focus on price as the most important factor, you will be respected more in Asia if you negotiate
well. More important, if you allow your counterpart (be it a
client or supplier) to negotiate well, they will have an elevated
status within their own organization. We touched on this in
our discussion of relationships in Asia, and I am aware that
most people in Western countries struggle to negotiate with
friends, but negotiation is a part of the Asian culture; in fact,
it is a sign of respect. You may go out and destroy someone in
a negotiation in the morning and that evening go out drinking
and celebrating your friendship.

We tell our clients that their Asian customers will often
negotiate with them for two to three weeks—even after they
receive payment. By this, I mean that no sale is ever final,
even when they have received the product or service and have
paid for it. While this may be a slight exaggeration, it deliv-
ers on the point I am trying to make: From day one until the
end of any transaction, negotiations on price, quality, delivery
dates—on everything—will continue. Being prepared for the
negotiation is half the battle; the other half is knowing what
your counterpart will negotiate. Will they send you an inferior
product? Will they try to pay less for your products? Will they
come back to you and say they cannot make the agreed upon
deadlines? Knowing this ahead of time will allow you to prepare and, with any luck, be able to address these negotiation
tactics.

A common story heard from companies that outsource
manufacturing to Asia is that they run a few small test
batches, get very good quality, and move forward with their
initial order. Again, they receive very good quality. The next
order is a little bigger, but this time the quality is not quite as
good (I call this the "silent negotiation," testing the company
to decide whether they will keep to their initial quality standards). Some companies send back the products and demand
a higher quality (the correct response); others do not send it

back, indicating that it is okay, it is good enough. Those who send it back typically have set the quality standard and this is the end of the issue. But, for those who don't return the product, the next order tends to come back even a little worse, followed by the next order, that is a little worse, and so on, until they either stand up and say this is unacceptable or change vendors. If this is the case, I can only hope they have learned a valuable lesson.

These stories ring true. Occasionally, the issue is quality; occasionally, it is schedule. It is important to recognize that this is as much a part of the negotiation as sitting at a table and deciding on a price.

3. *Misunderstanding the Function of Contracts and the Signing Ceremony*

A signing ceremony is a very common occurrence in Asia and should not to be taken lightly. A friend who ran the international sales training of a major software firm told me that they signed more contracts in China than in any other market in the world; yet, they struggled to turn a profit. Before he completed his sentence, I assumed these were annual or multiyear contracts and that this meant their sales and, hopefully, their profitability in China was one of the highest of anywhere in the world to match the number of contracts. He then explained that instead of annual contracts or multiyear contracts with their clients, they were forced to sign quarterly or semiannual contracts. My friend's company received no real benefit from these contracts, but they allowed their clients to show a new signing ceremony and, on rare occasions, to attempt to renegotiate their terms.

Asian cultures are built around being social and building relationships and the signing ceremony process demonstrates that two sides came together in agreement. Thus, when you are in Asia, a lot of photos are taken showing that you were there (although I always wonder where these photos end up, because I never see them). The irony is that the contract is really just a guide, so why do you need it in the first place? The answer, of course, is the relationship you build over the ceremony itself.

4. *Misinterpreting the Role of Capitalism in Communist Countries*

This relates more to China than anywhere else in Southeast Asia. China is obviously a communist country, but on an individual basis, the people you come across are capitalists first. When working in China you find that communism is of the utmost importance from the government's perspective. Because the government and the SOEs make up so much of the business sector in China, I do not mean that everyone ignores communism; that is not the case in the least. But private business people focus on capitalism and find ways to turn profits, above all else.

For years, SOEs completely dominated the business landscape in China, but in recent years that has evolved. The lack of profits and the primary focus of employing and providing for the masses have changed; and the government has spun off several SOEs as competition has increased.

Unable to compete because of their size and inability to adapt, the Chinese government has instead chosen to sell pieces, either in whole or in part, making the units or even the complete business a private entity that operates with a capitalist mindset and the goal of profitability. As changes continue, the economy is becoming more market-based with fewer and fewer state-owned monopolies.

Of course, communism is not the norm for all countries in Asia, even if some groups still operate in ways similar to the SOEs of China. The Benami system in India, a term used in Hindu law to designate a transaction, contract, or property that is made or held under a name that is fictitious or is that of a third party who holds as ostensible owner for the principle or beneficial owner, is a good example.[2] For years,

---

[2] http://www.merriam-webster.com/dictionary/benami

the profitability of the company was not the focus. This has shifted somewhat (although variations of the Benami system still exist in India), and in many ways the difference between the Benami system, which focused on lining the pockets of the elite political families, and the state-owned enterprises, which focused on employment, allowed an outsider to understand the motivations behind the business operations.

What is true is capitalism tends to reign and markets adjust to it. It does not matter if you are in Indonesia, Vietnam, South Korea, China, or India. It is important that Westerners understand that the businesses in these countries want to grow, they want to turn a profit, and they want to be the best.

5.   *Ignoring the Importance of "Gambe"*
This may not seem like it has economic value, but be prepared to drink alcohol. If you do not drink, feel free to tell your hosts; most will understand and will switch to tea and drink tea all night with you. Still, be prepared to toast, just with lots of tea drinking. Another important point, in China: If you are driving, let people know you are driving. There's great opposition in China to drinking and driving—even one drink is frowned upon. Yet, in many Asian cultures, sharing a long dinner with more drinks than you need is something of a rite of passage. Drinking with your counterparts is a way of doing business; it is celebrating your relationship and the potential of future business together. If you are the driver, it is typically very acceptable to drink tea with everyone instead of liquor.

What does this have to do with economic value? Besides the fact that this is a cost of doing business, gambe is also a value system in which you are judged by how well you celebrate your relationship. Turning your back on this custom can kill a deal faster than overpricing or a poor product. There will be a lot of toasts, and you will need to respond by toasting your hosts, just as they will toast to you. In years past, this was a negotiation tactic, where four or five local businessmen would gather around and, one at a time, toast with you.

So, for every four or five shots you did, they did one. As this process progressed, they would renegotiate your contract and, come 8:00 a.m., have a revised agreement ready for you to sign; an agreement you made over too many shots of shoju (in Korea), sake (in Japan), or baiju (in China). Thankfully, today this is much more a social practice than a negotiating tactic. So, when the time comes, "gambe" (which roughly translated means, "to the bottom").

Specific economic values change and evolve, as in the example of baby formula used above, but many of the inherent, broad-based market values remain fairly constant, as in negotiations and relationships. It is very important to recognize whether something is a specific or broad-based economic value because one can be changed and one cannot, at least not by one individual or one company. Your internal, economic values framework should be focused on several factors, including who you are as a company, what the market values as a whole, what the market values for your products or services, and what the people you are dealing with value. If you can encapsulate all of these into your own internal economic values framework, you will be well prepared to make your product or service offering, as well as adjust, if needed, in the future, whether in this market or the next.

CHAPTER 3

The Role Culture Plays in Determining Values and Ethical Standards and Practices

When I was raising money to start FDI Strategies, several investors asked about bribery in China. I told them, "I do not want to go to jail in the United States and I REALLY do not want to go to jail in China."

When people think of ethics and Southeast Asia, the first thing some people think of is bribery. I often remind our U.S. clients that the lines between bribery and an acceptable business interaction are very arbitrary, but as arbitrary as they are, they exist, and anyone doing business in Southeast Asia needs to protect their company and themselves from issues that could arise.

I call these lines arbitrary because in the United States, we would not judge a company negatively if a representative took a potential client out for a very expensive dinner or to a private luxury box to enjoy a football or basketball game. Despite the fact that this could add up to tens of thousands of dollars, we think nothing of it. Yet, if the representative had handed the potential client this money in cash, it would be illegal. Think of it as dating. You may buy dinner and flowers for your date, but if you simply offer cash, it implies something entirely different. So, I reiterate, these are arbitrary lines, but these arbitrary lines can get you in a lot of trouble, so pay attention to them.

Almost everyone has heard stories of bribery in China or India and, for that matter, throughout Southeast Asia. For years this had been a common practice, more so in some countries than others. In recent years, though, in the more established countries, this custom has decreased quite a bit, especially in China. Some cite China's growing acceptance of Western practices; others point to the country's leaders for cracking down on the practice. Either way, there has been a distinct focus on eliminating this longstanding practice. However, even though it is getting better, this does not mean bribery has been totally eliminated. It is very hard to completely eliminate a staple of a culture in just a few years. It will take diligence and fortitude for years to come in order to completely resolve the problem.

Caveat Emptor: Meet Before Getting Married

Here are a few personal stories, offered as examples of what to look for, both historically and today.

My first trip to China was to set up offices in Shanghai for a large museum design project we were awarded. As we explored this opportunity, we discovered several ways to make the office setup more than viable. We began looking for in-country fabricators as partners. The first fabricator I met with told me that it would be no problem to win three or four projects that we had initially focused on, but that we would need a $1 million marketing budget. My initial thought was, "What the hell would we need a $1 million marketing budget for? These projects would only provide about $5 million in total revenue." Before I could get the words out of my mouth, I realized what he was actually saying. Fortunately, I cut myself off from saying something I should not, and we were able to move forward with another partner.

At this time, I was new to China. Although we already had an office in Singapore for several years, Singapore operates with a lot of Western practices that hold back most conversations like that one. It was quite an eye opener for me that someone would boldly bring this up in an initial meeting; in China for only 24 hours, I had already been asked for a bribe. Luckily, we had lots of other potential partners to work with, and that allowed us to make sure we found good, strong partners that operated in an appropriate manner.

Companies in the United States have been lured into a relationship by someone who reaches out to them from China, supposedly for a large purchase or seeking a joint venture. In this type of situation, the U.S. company does some peripheral research and finds the company reaching out to them appears legitimate. So, after weeks or even months of working through details, everything seems to have lined up and they believe the order or joint venture is ready to be signed (without ever meeting the other party). At the last minute, the Chinese party notifies them of some issues that have arisen that can be cleared up for $5,000 or $10,000. While we may laugh because the scam seems so transparent, after weeks or months of effort, you might be surprised to hear how many companies come up with the money; after all, it's only $5,000 or $10,000 and this project could be worth millions. Needless to say, it does not work out.

Returning to the dating analogy, this is similar to an arranged marriage where no one on your side has a say in who you would marry. Looking at this through the lens of a joint venture, make sure you know who you are "getting in bed" with. Meaning, go meet the person, see the offices, and so on. If you are making a large business decision, which could include a large sale, a trip to China is justified. Think of it this way: A $1,500 flight and three nights at a hotel is cheaper than the $5,000 to $10,000 you just spent, which yielded nothing more than anger and headaches.

How do bribery or scams relate to differences in ethical standards, one might ask. Bribery is illegal in the United States and, clearly, the scam is deceit, if not theft. However, in certain parts of Asia, bribery is or was commonplace, and some in Asia may view the scam as shrewd negotiations, a characteristic that is seen as a great quality to be celebrated.

Five Ethical and Values Issues Businesses Encounter in Southeast Asia

The simple fact is that with any other culture, you cannot force your own values on them, nor should you try. What you can do is operate within your own principles and guidelines and make sure that you hold firm on these, even in a foreign country or dealing with another culture. This is hard to do, and some Americans have admitted to paying bribes in public forums because they felt that was the only way to succeed in foreign countries. These frequently related stories sometimes seem like "bribery bragging," something I cannot understand. In my experience, business can be done without paying bribes and compromising your own moral compass. You may not win every contract and it may take you a bit longer to succeed, but your success will come with the ability to sleep comfortably at night.

1. *Lying to Oneself: "I Had To Do It"*
I have attended conferences where people openly discuss the bribes they have paid. This is usually not because they are proud (perhaps some are proud to show their lumps) but because they want to show that there is no other choice. The truth of the matter is that we all have choices, all the time. Over the past 10+ years, many areas in Southeast Asia have

matured to a point where bribery is not the common practice anymore, or at least is becoming less and less common. President Xi Jinping of China has done a remarkable job of reducing and removing corruption within the Chinese government, and that is having a trickle-down effect on state-owned enterprises and flowing down to private businesses.

Something surprising to me is how often I hear people speak of something that is known to be illegal, and we are not talking about telling someone you were doing 65 mph in a 55 mph zone. Often, people justify their actions by assuming it is a one-time cost of entry—but it is rarely a one-time payment. In the United States, the *Foreign Corrupt Practices Act (FCPA)* is very clear about the penalties for this:

1. A. Any domestic concern that is not a natural person and that violates subsection (a) or (i) of this section shall be fined not more than $2,000,000.

   B. Any domestic concern that is not a natural person and that violates subsection (a) or (i) of this section shall be subject to a civil penalty of not more than $10,000 imposed in an action brought by the Attorney General.

2. A. Any natural person that is an officer, director, employee, or agent of a domestic concern, or stockholder acting on behalf of such domestic concern, who willfully violates subsection (a) or (i) of this section shall be fined not more than $100,000 or imprisoned not more than 5 years, or both.

   B. Any natural person that is an officer, director, employee, or agent of a domestic concern, or stockholder acting on behalf of such domestic concern, who violates subsection (a) or (i) of this section shall be subject to a civil penalty of not more than $10,000 imposed in an action brought by the Attorney General.

3. Whenever a fine is imposed under paragraph (2) upon any officer, director, employee, agent, or stockholder of a domestic concern, such fine may not be paid, directly or indirectly, by such domestic concern.[1]

- *The takeaway:* Find the right partners and the right in-country team. By "in-country team," I mean both your employees in a foreign country as well as your advisors.

Make sure that the people you surround yourself with have your best interests in mind. This may mean more vetting of your advisors than you might typically do, but this vetting process will pay long-term dividends, both in terms of peace of mind and future opportunity. As the economy changes, operating in the right way, and being well known to operate in the right way, can become a true asset.

I also recommend that companies think carefully about who they are sending over to lead their operations. If you send over an expatriate known for bending the rules to meet and break sales goals, you are probably setting yourself up for failure or, worse yet, fines and jail time. Such people have justified the way they have bent the rules for years, and expecting them to act differently in a foreign country would be foolish.

- *The takeaway:* Rule benders will be rule benders. Sometimes, it is not in your best interest to send someone with the highest sales record, or who moves very quickly.

2. *Avoiding the Issue: "Let's Not Go There"*
People often find that the best way to deal with ethical or bribery issues is to avoid the country or opportunity as a whole, but just because you might encounter difficult ethical issues does not mean you should avoid doing business in that

---

[1] https://www.justice.gov/sites/default/files/criminal-fraud/legacy/2012/11/14/fcpa-english.pdf

country. Instead, it's important to figure out if you can operate successfully without bribery.

Research is a good way to figure this out. View other U.S, companies and how they operate in that country. U.S. companies even sell in a country like North Korea, so you are not the first.

- *The takeaway:* Learn from those who did it before you, learn from their successes and failures, and figure out how to do it better.

Let your principles dictate *how* you do business, but do not let them decide whether or not you do business. By reviewing the country's codes of ethics and also examining how the business environment actually operates, you may find opportunities to do business ethically. Even in India where the Benami system—where government officials act on behalf of the family and thus the family-owned company is effectively a state business—forces you out of certain relationships (it would be foolish to think a government will buy from you as opposed to the governor's brother), there may yet be privately held businesses willing to do business with an outsider who offers them something better.

Similar to a monopoly system, a system with poor regulation of corruption discourages innovation (most people assume it is easier to bribe someone than to innovate new products and services). Look for ways to take advantage of existing systems and find ways to beat the system. When you can clearly define the problem in the society, you can't develop a strategy and plan to beat it.

3.   *Partnering for Cover: "Let the Other Guy Do It"*
Doing illegal things through a partner is still illegal. Do not think that just because you didn't issue the payment, you are not liable. What you need to do is make sure you truly vet your partners; this includes joint ventures, outsourced sales teams, law and accounting firms, among others. There is

definitely guilt by association, so make sure your associations provide no room for doubt, no grey area for guilt. It's important that you find out how your partner does business and how they built their business. You and no one else are responsible for whom you do business with. The fact that the person or business you are doing business with is not from the United States, and not held to the FCPA, does not mean much when you are dealing with the U.S. government.

- *The takeaway:* Err on the safe side, proceed with caution, and find ways to make sure you can, and should, trust the people you are doing business with. Go out and speak to other clients and suppliers of the people you are doing business with and screen them in the same way you might screen a new employee. And follow their customs of close personal relationships. The better you get to know someone, the more likely you are to know how they will act in different scenarios.

4. *Imposing Their Values on Another Culture: Sexism, Racism, Ageism, and Other –Isms*

This is a tough one. In the United States, we operate in ways that encourage diversity and fair play. Fairness is not always achieved, but there are many ways to level the playing field—federal and state laws, business best practices, for example. Programs like the Minority Owned Business Enterprises (MBE) and Woman Owned Business Enterprises (WBE) allow businesses to grow and offer opportunities. Likewise, businesses in the United States continue to focus on issues such as having women and/or minorities on corporate boards of directors and in senior leadership roles.

On the other hand, it is important to remember that many of these U.S. programs are not that old, perhaps 50 years at the oldest. In other countries, especially in Asia, these programs are perhaps 10 years in place. Expecting them to accelerate through the system in this time frame is near impossible.

But, it is important to take notice and pay attention to the changes taking place, as well as encourage these changes in the communities where you work. Already there is a female in the Chinese Politburo. Could there be more? Of course, but that will take time, and I've no doubt the situation will improve in the future.

If the issue of women's or minority rights has only become a concern in the past five or 10 years, and previously women or minorities held only low-level jobs, it is unrealistic to expect large numbers of them to move into upper management overnight. If someone has risen two or three levels in the past five years, that is progress, and a way of getting to where things should be. So, it is better to judge the system on where it is going than where it is.

Another important thing to keep in mind here is the part you can play in moving this change forward. Hiring the best people is always the key, but keeping your own code of ethics is just as important. Perhaps equally important is recognizing these –isms, so that you can work with your team to not only protect your staff, but also encourage growth in your local employees.

- *The takeaway:* If racism or sexism is still embedded in the country's culture, make sure you are acutely aware of that as you send your female general manager out into the market. Understand what repercussions may come up when she is trying to close a deal, and find a way to best support her as she moves forward and grows your operations. This can be done by assigning the appropriate title to elevate the status of the general manager—would "managing director" work better to elevate status? This can also be done by making sure she is seated in the dominant seat in the room, how she is respected by peers and even supervisors, and, most importantly, not giving the counterpart reason to second-guess her authority by casual jokes or having the wrong people accompany her to the meeting.

5. *Lacking Cultural Sensitivity and Tact: Freedom of Speech Is Not a Guarantee*

It is important to know the time and the place to broach these issues. Freedom of speech is not guaranteed in every country in the world. By asking someone about a topic in public and putting them on the spot, you may be jeopardizing their freedom, especially if the person answers incorrectly.

Recently, while traveling with a delegation in Shanghai, we were at the China Executive Leadership Academy in Pudong (CELAP), and one of the delegates asked why there were no women in the Chinese Politburo (not exactly accurate, but the person could be forgiven for missing the one woman member). The tour guide politely avoided answering the question, but the American still appeared a bit put off until I explained that a "wrong answer" might land the guide in jail. To my surprise, the tour guide, a relatively senior communist party member, brought the subject up later on and answered it very well and truthfully, explaining that women's rights had not been around for as long in China as they had been in the West, and that they were working on it.

I think this demonstrated two things: 1) that these issues are not going unnoticed, and 2) that the government was becoming more and more tolerant when it comes to freedom of speech.

- *The takeaway:* Keep this in mind when dealing with different groups in Asia, and remember there is a time and a place to ask questions, and putting someone on the spot in front of a large group is usually a bad idea and quite risky.

It still amazes me what some people will do to survive. In the United States, our rules and regulations are fairly clear. In some countries, laws may be more open to interpretation, but here the laws are out there and it's your choice whether you pay attention to them or not, and open yourself up to fines

or imprisonment. Beyond survival, it's important to understand and respect the country and citizens with whom you are
dealing. It's not fair to judge them based on your own ethics
and guidelines, just as it would not be fair for them to judge
you based on their ethics and guidelines. Find a way to work
within the confines of both, but also find a way to ask questions that will help you understand why things are done that
way; gather information and allow it to guide your thoughts
on the future of the country. Make sure you do it in private,
so you don't put the other person on the spot. Hopefully, the
answers you receive will show you a country that is evolving
and not devolving. I think it's safe to say that we have not
achieved full equality in the United States, despite trying for
over 50 years, so why should you assume that another country
should do it in 10? If you see a country in which you wish
to do business moving backward from the standpoint of ethics, assess the situation and consider how it applies to your
business.

CHAPTER 4

Gauging Market Potential: How to Spot Trends and Avoid Costly Errors

It's important to remember that market potential is just a guess; hopefully, it's an informed guess but, nonetheless, it's just a guess. Do not let your bias interfere with your decision-making process.

One of the most important parts of assessing market potential is your ability to spot trends that might apply to your products or services. Perhaps the easiest country in which to do this is China because of the specificity of the government's five-year plans. "After the founding of the People's Republic of China in 1949, there was an economic recovery period until 1952. Starting in 1953, the first Five-Year Plan was implemented. Except for a two-year hiatus for economic adjustment in 1963–1965, the Five-Year Plans have been continuous. The first five Five-Year Plans feature a Soviet command style economic model characterized by state ownership, farming collectives, and centralized economic planning. The Soviets even helped China craft its first Five-Year Plan."[1] A surprising revelation to those outside of China is that

---

[1] Quote from Lauren Mack - http://chineseculture.about.com/od/historyofchina/a/Chinese-History-Five-Year-Plan.htm

much of the prosperity in China is a result of the five-year plans, designed and implemented by the current president of the People's Republic of China, Xi Jinping, and the Politburo. The five-year plan covers how they will grow the economy and improve the country over the next five years. This sets the wheels in motion and businesses in China decide how to capitalize on the opportunities presented by the new plan.

In some instances, this doesn't provide the anticipated result. For example, an opportunity that seemed very attainable, but never progressed, is the development of clean coal plants. Part of the 12th and 13th five-year plans focused on clean air and, in a country that burns coal for almost all forms of heat and energy, clean coal seemed like a great opportunity. Not only was there a push from the government to switch, but there were subsidies making clean coal only slightly more expensive than the "dirty" coal that released carcinogens and other chemicals into homes, and undoubtedly shortened the life span of many people in China.

Why did this plan fail? Interestingly, clean coal does not put out the same amount of heat or have the same burn time, so families continued to purchase "dirty" coal because they couldn't afford to buy as much clean coal. Factories that converted coal sat at 10–25% use rates, so even after receiving subsidies for plant construction and the coal itself, it failed because people could not be forced to use the clean coal. Clearly, there was a need for clean air, there was government support, and most would have predicted a successful transition to a cleaner-burning coal that would have improved the lives of the citizens in China. However, to date we have not seen the switch occur.

With this said, there are many examples of companies capitalizing on the five-year plans as they go into effect. Most construction companies have seen immense growth over the last 10+ years in China because infrastructure growth has been a huge priority. Local and foreign companies alike have been able to take advantage of this for years; that is, the Zhongnan

Group has grown from relative obscurity to $3+ billion in revenues[2] and U.S. businesses, such as HDR Engineering, Inc.,[3] have worked on projects for public and private clients throughout China.

Sleuthing for Indicators of Market Potential

It's a bit harder to spot potential trends in other countries throughout Southeast Asia; but some of the principles remain the same. Working with the governments in Southeast Asia is a necessity. Large opportunities do not exist in Asia without government approval and support; therefore, finding ways to work with the government, especially if you are working on infrastructure projects, is a must.

So, how do you sleuth out the market potential, especially in societies that, unlike the United States and Europe, do not have easily accessible market information available? Certain countries in Southeast Asia are very protective of corporate information; similarly, certain countries' corporate information is less than trustworthy. So, how do you gauge your competition in the market? I recommend using several key indicators in a market to help establish information.

For example, for a client of ours, X-IO Technologies (a data storage company based in Colorado Springs, Colo.), we had two employees working in China, people with a very good knowledge of the industry. But when we explored growth, some of their assumptions turned out to be false because they hadn't targeted particular sectors they felt were unavailable to them, such as Chinese banks. Upon further research, we discovered quotes from the chief information officer (CIO) of the Bank of China stating they were using IBM, Oracle, and EMC for data storage despite a specific government push

---

[2] http://znjs.com/en/
[3] http://www.hdrinc.com/portfolio?region=298&market=All&keywords=

to move away from these three companies (this policy was known as Ex-IOE). The CIO stated that in order for them to provide the security and infrastructure necessary to operate as a major international bank, international firms, specifically these three, were the only options currently available.

The lesson here is to ensure you closely examine all of your assumptions. Our company's assumptions came from very intelligent, well-educated people who were on the ground working in the country. It's also important to remember that in every country there are sectors that foreign firms cannot participate in; for example, in the United States you would not see a Chinese defense contractor win a Department of Defense project. Make sure you figure out at an early stage, which sectors you can and cannot participate in. It's also important to keep an eye on evolving developments, as certain sectors open up to foreign businesses.

Key Indicator #1: Public Source Data

Public source data is not always available and not always reliable, but it's a start on your journey. Sources might include information from trade magazines, business publications in the country, and trade websites from the country of interest. The benefits to you of these sources are that they are relatively inexpensive and sometimes free, can be researched from your office or home, and a lot of information can be collected, compared, and contrasted quickly. The obvious downside is lack of reliability.

Key Indicator # 2: End-user Polling

A second source of information used by our company is end-user polling, which is especially helpful in finding pricing data, particularly if you are a business-to-business (B2B) firm that does not have a product on the shelf. On larger, more expensive items, this is a very valuable piece of information both for determining price, add-on features, and other changes that may be needed.

For example, the medical industry in Asia has changed rapidly over the last two decades. If your company is considering exporting your products and services to Asia, you might ask:

- Is your business handling alternative medicines, that is, herbal medicines that need a freshness seal rather than the traditional packaging used for pills and liquids?

- Is your business primarily with doctors' offices or hospitals? If hospitals, are they large with many beds, or small and typically involved in outpatient care? Is there a retail pharmacy on site, or do patients fill prescriptions at local retail pharmacies?

These are questions that our company looked to hospital administrators to answer for us. Typically, we can successfully find answers that cover what the current practices are, why they are being done, and where there are gaps by asking questions such as whether there is a benefit to manufacturing in the country and if so how that would be filled. This information is obviously relevant to the products and services that our client wishes to introduce.

A recent conversation with a source in India about a language software tool intended for hospital use did not produce the expected response. The 2001 India census found that there were 30 languages spoken by more than one million people; 122 languages by more than 10,000 people; and 1,599 other languages spoken in India. Obviously, communicating with patients can be a challenge. Nevertheless, this particular product was quickly dismissed by a top medical professional because it required broadband internet service, which was not available in much of India, and therefore the tool would be too costly for hospitals to access. Instead, the decision-makers believed it would be easier and cheaper to let the patients figure out what languages were spoken in their local hospital, and, if necessary, use the services of a translator via phone or in person.

Key Indicator #3: Conferences and Trade Shows

Great market research can be done at conferences and trade shows if you pay close attention and listen to the right people. Similar to public source data, you have to fact-check to ensure the information you receive is reliable. Venues like these can be great opportunities to speak directly with potential clients or suppliers or to hear what industry experts in the country say about where the particular markets you are interested in are going. It is also a good place to see who your competition is, if they really have a competitive product, and, perhaps, even what they are charging for it.

All of this information is essential to your exploration of market potential and will help you understand and determine what planes to compete on. For example:

- Are you selling a high quality product at a higher price?

- Are you competing on price?

- Are you competing on service?

Going back to X-IO Technologies: In the United States, they offer a superior product at a lower price than their competition. In the Chinese market, a lower price is usually associated with an inferior product. We encouraged them to raise their price in China and compete on their superior quality, which was prevention of downtime, a very important detail in corporate hardware systems.

Key Indicator # 4: In-country Market Research Firms

Although more expensive, in-country market research firms can provide very detailed data. If you are looking to cut costs, they often are not the answer, but if you have the resources, they are a great way to get very detailed reports on all of your data points. The price differential is pretty significant between in-country, local firms, and international firms, so it is possible to find less expensive options that can still provide good research. These firms provide pieces of all of the three methods discussed above, and, if they are good, do it in a more efficient, effective way than your company could using its own time and effort.

Five Common Mistakes Companies Make When Researching Market Potential

When analyzing the market potential for your business, you need to review the opportunities, the threats, and what is happening in the market. You can do this in a variety of ways at various costs—monetary costs, time costs, and quality of information—but the important thing is that you make sure you do them; the penalties for not doing so can be the difference between success and failure. Here are five key errors and how you can avoid making them.

1. *Developing a Biased View of Market Potential as a Result of Insufficient Research*
Doing some online research paired with questioning a few sources and justifying this method by saying we did not have the time or resources for a long, drawn-out study—In my experience, this means someone does a Google search and talks to a few friends in the United States who have experience in the market. What does this typically create? A very biased view of the market.

It is probably fair to say that no one person knows everything about a specific market. For instance, a person who has lived and worked in the United States their whole life, and worked in many different cities across the United States, could make a lot of assumptions, but that person might still overlook many opportunities in specific areas that are unknown to them or misunderstood because the person doesn't have specific knowledge of that particular area or product. The same holds true for Asia. On the other hand, if you know someone who is really insightful about a particular market, keep that person close.

When looking at a country in Asia, do not rely on a few friends and a Google search to provide adequate information. At the very least, include a search of local media sources. In addition, talk to your law firm and accounting firm. They may have a partner or office in the country; if so, ask them to establish contact for your company. This would be an appropriate source of input, and making a phone call will be worth the time and resources.

> *The takeaway:* Taking the path of least resistance rarely produces the desired outcome.

2. *Not Adjusting Properly for Risk*
Here's an example of what I mean: Some Americans make certain assumptions about a market; if it is a large market, we assume it will stay that way. To Americans, it is almost incomprehensible to think that railroads would be deemed government property or that they would be taken over by the federal government. However, in some countries, such as Russia, historically, the government has played a large role in the ownership of railroads.

> *The takeaway:* Do not assume all countries operate in the same way.

A false sense of security can develop, and a company may be caught off guard, for example, when a government unexpectedly changes its policies, as the Chinese government did when they adopted the Ex-IOE policy,[4] which required government offices and state-owned enterprises to show cause to use software other than those mandated by the state.

---

[4] http://www.marketwatch.com/story/china-pulling-the-plug-on-ibm-oracle-others-2014-06-26

There are always risks, and often they are much more prevalent than we immediately understand. A great recent example concerns universities in the United States that recruit Chinese students, who are seen as high-quality students who paid full tuition and represent an almost endless supply of future students, given the enormous population of China. But two things have occurred that could change the success rate of this recruitment program: 1) students returning to China after graduation have found it increasingly difficult to find jobs, especially jobs paying salaries that can justify having paid 30 to 50 times more tuition than if they had gone to school in China (Chinese tuition runs between roughly $1,000 and $2,500 per year). The cost is not only monetary. During the Chinese student's absence, he or she has also lost relationship-development time. 2) Another factor is now in play; the Chinese government recently stated that if you want to rise to a high government position, you must have studied in China. It remains to be seen how this will affect the decisions of Chinese students thinking of coming to the United States and Europe; this will have no effect on students who wish to stay in the United States and Europe after they graduate.

> *The takeaway:* Anticipate the unexpected.

Are there Asian markets where this is less of an issue? Japan has less market risk than other countries in the region, but they are very protective of their markets. Singapore is perhaps the most open to outsiders, having a lot of work performed by companies from other countries. This mainly stems from the fact that their economy is built around shipping and trade, and thus they have always been open to foreign enterprises.

3.   *Not Paying Enough Attention to Local Competition*
Some companies in the United States minimize the impact of competition that does not play directly into the same price or quality category as their product(s) because they do not

view it as direct competition. Does Ferrari consider Vespa their direct competitor in the United States? Of course not. Should they consider it in developing their strategy in the U.S. market? Yes.

In emerging economies, it is easy for priorities to shift and changes to occur quickly. For example, even though the high-end electric vehicle market in China had little competition, recently several companies have stepped in because of subsidies and their need to seek growth markets.

As a result of increased taxes on traditional vehicles and the elimination of these taxes on electric vehicles in an attempt to encourage less exhaust pollution in Chinese cities, many companies have quickly come into the electric car market. Today, there may not be a one-to-one comparison with Tesla, but it may not be long before there is direct competition.

In the United States, some might consider it extremely costly and unlikely for a new company to compete with Tesla, but, then again, it was not that long ago that Tesla took the risk with substantial backing from Elon Musk. This relates to imposing our own values on a foreign culture. We see building a factory and developing a business as too costly to justify the process, but in emerging markets, different factors motivate them (glance back at chapter 2 and the discussion of economic values for a refresher, if necessary). Emerging markets can garner worldwide market share because profits are not the sole, or even the primary, motivator.

Look at India, which over the past two decades has seen its economy morph from one almost monopolized by a handful of private companies and state-run companies to an environment in which many new companies keep appearing. In the past, a business person would have looked at and only vetted the several private companies and state-run companies as probable competition. The state-run companies, traditionally, ran at a loss and subsidized the cost of what they produced for the people of India.

> ➤ *The takeaway:* For a company thinking of investing in Asia, ignoring today's realities and the fact that growth has happened throughout Asia could be fatal.

4. Not Understanding What Part of the Market You Can, and Will, Capture

Nothing happens instantaneously, and, for this reason, initially our company will often target microsegments of a sector to build up a brand reputation; ideally these segments are made up of fast-growing sectors that are in need of new developments, such as our client's technology. A great example of this is X-IO Technologies. When we were looking at market growth, we targeted, among other areas, social media applications. Social media applications obviously need a storage environment and cannot afford downtime. They need zero failure rates, and that is what X-IO offers because of its advanced engineering technology. Consider the movie *The Social Network*, when Mark Zuckerberg is yelling at Eduardo Saverin, "We are never down, we can't go down even for one minute." If a social site is down for one minute or one hour, their traffic migrates to another option. Thus, downtime can be fatal since there are so many options.

Once we capture a microsegment, we then use this market capture to grow into other segments. We were fortunate that in China, social networks are growing into many new sectors, including banking and retail among others, so there was built-in growth as well, even among the initial target client set. We used small segments as a stepping-stone into a larger market.

> ➤ *The takeaway:* Use a stepped approach to growth into a new market, hitting new plateaus each year and steadily increasing market presence, pairing it with your costs to eliminate unnecessary overhead early on, while attempting to maximize your growth potential for the future.

5.   *Forgetting Your Established Clients at Home*

When looking at the market potential in Asia, you may find that your current clients are already established there. If you sell to Walmart in the United States, it would be prudent to contact their international division and attempt to get into their stores in the foreign markets you are entering. Likewise, if you sell to law firms or accounting firms, make sure they are using your products in the foreign markets. Also consider organizations you partner with and anyone else you can tie in. Too often, when looking at market potential, valuable work you've previously done is overlooked.

A glaring example of this particular oversight emerged during a conversation with an Asian subsidiary of a U.S. client and the company's managing director of Asia. The managing director told me his relationship with headquarters was positive, but also said that he had never met his boss in person, and that they did not share information across the company. For example, our client had no idea who the company's clients were in the United States, Australia, Europe, or anywhere else. Likewise, other than his boss, no one on the sales team in those countries outside of Asia knew who his clients were either.

My first piece of advice to this company about growing their sales was to share your client list (they looked at me as if I had discovered a cure for cancer). Although, I was caught off guard the first time I heard this story, I do not believe it will be the last time. As an organization, you have worked hard to bring in clients in your geographic area; therefore, it is important to maximize their potential. That client chose you in your home market for a reason, and usually that reasoning will apply across borders, making for an easier sales opportunity than a completely new client would.

> ➤ *The takeaway:* Do not forget simple things, like working with your current clients; they could be your best entry into a new market.

At the end of the day, remember market potential for your business is a forecast, which essentially means it's a "best guess" on a spreadsheet to pass through everyone's hands. It may well be an "educated best guess," but be prepared to adjust as needed. And remember, as you prepare it, try not to make assumptions informed by your own biases. It's very easy to do, and sometimes hard to catch, but inevitably these assumptions will either set goals too high or bring down your foreign operations by improper expectations. These assumptions can be market based, company based, or competition based. No matter what these assumptions relate to, you'll need to keep an unbiased eye on them to make sure you have some checks and balances.

CHAPTER 5

Understanding the Power Structure: Who's *Really* in Charge?

Power tends to corrupt and absolute power corrupts absolutely.   Sir John Dalberg-Acton

Just like in other countries, in Asia a power structure exists within a country and it is up to you to understand how it functions. For instance, in China, you have state-owned enterprises; in Japan, there are the Keidanren, a Japanese business federation made up of companies, industrial associations, and regional economic organizations; India has the Benami, where old families, such as Tata, rule the roost. Needless to say, in all of these countries, there are dominating forces that have a stranglehold on the overall business community and an ability to keep their power. It's very important to learn who these groups are, what their interests are, and how to work with them (or, if you cannot work with them, how to stay below their radar). When I think of these groups, I am often reminded of a favorite line from a movie that most people probably never saw.

In the movie *The Great White Hype*, Samuel L Jackson plays a boxing promoter who has a stranglehold on the boxing world and oversees all the corruption within it. Cheech Marin plays the boxing commissioner. Jackson is trying to get him to rank a particular white boxer in the top 10 despite the fact that he has never fought a professional fight. The conversation goes like this:

> Jackson: "What will it take to get him ranked in the top 10...Money?"
> Marin: "No."
> Jackson: "Sex?"
> Marin: "No."
> Jackson: "Drugs?"
> Marin:"No."
> Jackson: Pauses for a moment, and says, "Power?"
> Marin: "Yeah, power."
> Jackson: "You're fired."
> Marin: "Okay, money, sex, and drugs."

My point is not to cite lines from a movie many people never saw, but, instead, to highlight the analogous role played by these groups in foreign countries. Just as Jackson has the power to fire Marin, they have the power and the relationships, and they have worked through them for years and years, to do as they please.

As a newcomer, you have to navigate this arena and ask yourself what you want. Do you want sales, sales and profits, long-term growth? You will not be able to get them all today. What do you want today and what do you want tomorrow? Working with the large groups that rule the country's economy, you'll be able to ask for it piece by piece, and not have it all ripped away from you with just two words, as Cheech Marin's character did.

All of the power groups, those mentioned above and others, have some common characteristics. They are large in both revenues and power, they are the government or have strong government ties, they easily navigate the currents in their own countries, and they have growing power outside their own countries.

Their composition is always changing and power is constantly shifting. They still have massive power, but, as Bob Dylan wrote, "the times, they are a changin'." To see where they are now and where they may be going, we'll examine each of them.

Chinese State-Owned Enterprises (SOEs)

There are roughly 200 SOEs in China. At this point, they represent some of the largest businesses in the country and thus the world. These businesses have traditionally been owned and operated 100 percent by the Chinese government, and reported to it through the Ministry of Commerce (MOFCOM). Many of these companies operate in industries that have traditionally been blocked from outside interest, giving them a near monopoly in their sectors in China. Most of these companies were established within the last 50 years, and their focus was on keeping both jobs and revenues in China. Occasionally they were formed in an effort to create consumer trust. A great example is banking, which both people and businesses have not always trusted. Historically, banking, particularly in rural areas, was done through a "dark" market operated by supposedly trusted individuals in each community. State-owned banks gave people a reason to believe the government would stand behind their deposits.

Recently, the Chinese SOEs are starting to be broken up and turned into private companies.[1] The Chinese government is now saying "Enough" to these companies, which have dominated the Chinese landscape for years, operating at times without the requirement to make a profit. Through a variety of means, these companies are transitioning, sometimes as a joint venture with a private equity fund, sometimes filing an

---

[1] http://www.forbes.com/sites/kenrapoza/2015/12/30/china-starts-breaking-up-its-state-owned-enterprises/#61a2d23d56e5

initial public offering and garnering public interest. Regardless of method, they are moving away from being wholly owned by the Chinese government. With the advent of new private companies, a major reason for this shift in policy has been the SOEs' lack of performance. This does not mean that all SOEs are going away; in fact, even those that are becoming privatized will likely (at least initially) still be owned in part by the government.

Japan's Keidanren

"Keidanren" roughly translated means "Japan Business Federation," and has been in existence since 1946. Relatively speaking, this is the oldest organization of the three we are reviewing, but considering the long history of these countries, it is still relatively new. The Keidanren is made up of 1,329 representative companies, 109 nationwide industrial associations, and 47 regional economic organizations.[2] The purpose of the Keidanren is to organize the country's business, maximize the growth of industries, and make sure that Japan competes on a global scale. The leaders of this organization come from some of the most well-known Japanese companies in the world. The Keidanren also makes sure that there is a consensus in the business community on certain domestic and international issues. It's with all of this in mind that one finds the true power of the Keidanren, as it functions as guardian of the Japanese economy.

I recently met with the Japanese Keidanren and some of its most important directors, and found, as one might expect, they are a very formal organization—everything comes from a script and rules are followed, but they are very focused on driving growth and open to improving the Japanese economy,

---

[2] http://www.keidanren.or.jp/en/profile/pro001.html

and for this reason they will listen when the right people speak and work to advance the Japanese economy.

India's Benami[3]

We have seen significant changes in the power structure in India over the last 25 years and it's important to understand this history when trying to understand its economy. Prior to 1991, everything was licensed; the system was 100 percent patronage based, and only a few families made it big, similar to the Russian oligarchs and the Soviet system. At that time, state enterprises were in every business sector and they thrived, not by making profits, but with sales.

After 1991, there was a systemic change and the government not only removed most of the license system, but they also attempted to get out of most businesses. Families still held their power; but politicians effectively took large parts of the economy for themselves and put someone in charge of a business so they could siphon the profits off for themselves (this was called Benami). Benami is defined as someone, or some entity, that acts on behalf of a powerful patron, the ultimate beneficiary of the relationship being the patron. Every politician's family members owned factories, businesses, and corporations that secured government contracts and projects, and were given advance knowledge of impending policy changes.

Today things have changed somewhat, but not as much as in Japan or China. Families still make up the elite and old families such as Tata, Birla, Ambani, Bajaj, and Godrej are still quite powerful. Many of these still have family members who are politicians, that is, at least one member is a politician, even if the rest are businesspeople.

---

[3] All information directly from Dr. Ashley Miholi

But now new families are rising up to the elite, families such as Adani, Maran, Reddy, Mittal, and Jindal, most of which are not Benami but rather beneficiaries of the pre-1991 license raj (or governmental rules). Even without the Benami in your family, you still need the government to get things done and these families also have ties to every political party. Thus, as one political party rises to power, their families rise to power in business, and the other families go into hibernation, waiting until their politicians return to power. Corruption in India still runs rampant and ill-gotten wealth is taken out of India by overinvoicing imports. It's then routed back into India by foreign direct investment taking advantage of tax havens.

SOEs, Keidanren, and Benami are three examples of how some of the largest economies in Asia operate; similar systems exist in almost every country, if not every country, in Asia. Looking at them, you can see that there's great benefit to working with, instead of against, these organizations, especially as you try to grow your business in one of these countries.

At the same time, it's also helpful to understand that there have been changes over the years and, as you view each of these societies, it's important to recognize the direction in which they are moving. If the direction of the organization is plotted, hopefully your company can profit from it. When talking about direction, you might examine why the Chinese SOEs are being turned into privately owned businesses. On the surface, there are obvious reasons like lack of profitability and a shift of governmental priorities, but dig deeper and you find there are also issues with corruption that is being rooted out of the government. If the Chinese government wanted to eliminate rampant corruption within an organization that they owned, they could either arrest everyone or simply divest the government of the business and make it someone else's problem. They seem to have chosen the latter road.

So while it's extremely important to recognize the powers that be, their direction, and their interests, it's also important to know how to work around them. This is not to say that you should completely ignore them; however, if you're operating in a country where the institutions of power are corrupt, keeping up ties and perhaps sales while operating without them becoming a large part of your business is of utmost importance.

Five Common Mistakes Businesses Make When Confronted with the Power Structure of a Southeast Asian Country

Whether you are working with the SOEs of China, the Keidanren of Japan, the Benami of India, or the "power" in any other Asian country, it's important to understand the power structure of that country to avoid mistakes that can lead to failure.

Most of us in the West can easily cite differences in how business is done between the United States and England, but the differences among the countries of Asia are significant. There have been books written about the power elites of Asian countries, just as there have been books about the historically powerful families in the United States and England. If working with the government or these families is imperative to your business success, as it is to any business that wants to grow, it's essential that you make sure you understand how the power is distributed and who you need to work with in that country or countries to gain power and have your voice heard.

The other important thing to remember if you want to be successful is to pay attention to how the power changes and what creates these changes. Is it only during changes of leadership in the country that power changes? Perhaps even this does not change the real "powers" that you are beholden to. The change doesn't have to be extremely drastic for there to be opportunities in Asian markets. Changes in the power structure occur throughout Asian countries; for example, when looking at India, voting changes opportunities; when looking at China, opportunities become abundant every time there is a new five-year plan installed. Look for key determinants that trigger change and use them to anticipate and exploit market change. Sometimes country operations will adapt to these power changes, such as the five-year plans in China, and sometimes you might find exploitable factors that are not being focused on in the country. Both can be very profitable, but the latter may offer the most opportunity with the least competition.

1. *Believing They Do Not Need Help Setting Up a Business in the Country*

Building a relationship in Southeast Asia and penetrating into a country's elite requires an introduction. Using your state and federal government relationships is the best way to make your way into these foreign federations. Find ways to attend trade delegations with state and federal organizations that often include meetings with SOEs in China and the Keidanren of Japan; make sure you maximize your opportunities during these times. It's not easy, especially in Japan where you will be in very formal meetings.

For the most part, the majority of Southeast Asian countries maintain very formal meeting practices. Find ways to make those meetings stick; for example, be the only American at the table who shares a business card with the Chinese (Japanese, etc.) translation on the back—make sure the translation is correct; take the time to learn their traditions, to learn a few simple phrases like "hello" or "thank you," or a traditional toast. These small gestures show that you care, that you want to do business with them, and that you are coming for the long term. Instead of trying to avoid the powers of the country, make a point of getting to know them. As you get to know them, good employees may come to work with you who have useful contacts, and there may be opportunities for you to team up as businesses. Contrariwise, you never know if they will remain the powers they are (see the discussion above about the privatization of China's SOEs).

Perhaps a good way to think about this is to ask yourself, would you avoid the Fortune 100 in the United States? More than likely, your answer is, "No, I would seek them out." Why would this change in a foreign market just because of their governmental relationships? Their relationships with other local businesses? The operations may be different, motives may be changing, but your goal is to make sure that you are seeking opportunities for growth.

2. *Believing the Country Is Big Enough to Ignore the Nation's Power Structure*

Make no mistake about it: No matter how big the country is, you want to pursue all of it. Maybe not on day one, maybe not on day two, but you need to find your opportunities throughout the whole country and that undoubtedly means doing business with whoever holds the power in that country. Too often, companies think the market is big enough for everyone; however, when it comes to Southeast Asia, it's critical that you understand that only the strong survive. To make it in the market, you need to be able to maximize your business.

The Chinese Railroad System is a great example of the importance of maintaining relationships and the ability to grow one's business. For years, this system was extremely corrupt. Then, in 2015, one of the biggest corruption cases in China's history was exposed, and Liu Zhijun, the former minister of the railways, was sentenced to death for bribery and abuse of power.[4] As a business leader in China who worked with the railroads and transportation industries, I saw a new lifeline for business open up, and being a first mover was imperative.

---

[4] http://www.theguardian.com/world/2013/jul/08/liu-zhijun-sentenced-death-corruption

Businesses that were previously nearly banished from these sectors were now able to take on new business opportunities. Prior to the shift in China, we had continued to pursue opportunities, albeit in smaller areas or smaller projects. This gave our clients needed exposure, relationships with influential people, and early growth. When the power shifted, it opened up floodgates of opportunities that were not there before.

3. *Not Having the Right "Power" Relationships*

This one is harder to gauge because you could be working with someone at an SOE or in the Keidanren, and it might not be the right relationship. You have to figure out how much true power the person has in the organization because if that person does not have power, they aren't going to admit it. They will try to use their relationship with you to gain more power inside their own organization; you may just be along for the ride.

Situations like this have been seen time and again in China: A U.S. businessman wanders into the airport in full-on celebratory mode. He has just secured a major contract and wants to make sure everyone knows. After working for six months with the vice president, the contract is signed and the businessman will return to the United States to make sure everyone knows it was their hard work and persistence that got this done. What the person does not realize is that, typically, in China, only one person can sign and chop. It's required for a contract to be legally binding contract, and 99.9% of the time, the person is not a vice president. At best, in China, contracts are merely guidelines, but if the right person has not signed and chopped them, they're worth less than the paper they are printed on. It is essential when doing business in China that you make sure you are working with the right person. Having the right relationships will allow you to ask around to ensure you are in talks with the right person.

In addition, the right relationships give you access to the right people. Having strong relationships to build information around is a key piece to success in Asian markets.

4. *Believing the Power Structure Doesn't Play in Their Market*

It's foolish to think that you're in a highly profitable arena and that the country's elite businesses haven't taken notice. It's possible that your technology is so new and great that they're not in your business right now, but how long do you think that will last? Companies with money and power tend not to cede ground forever. In sports, we often say a great defense is a good offense. In simple terms, if you are out pushing forward at all times, do you think they can catch up with you? Can you get out in front of the elite organizations and build your relationship with them so that they decide not to invade your space and, perhaps, instead become dependent upon you? This happens more often than people realize.

If it's easier and cheaper for these elite-owned large companies to purchase from you than to develop the technology themselves, they may continue to purchase it from you. Usually, this will not last forever, but options like an Original Equipment Manufacturer (OEM)[5] or a joint venture may be an alternative for the future. Your initial strategy does not have to be your strategy forever; you should be constantly reviewing and updating it, looking for ways to better develop the market, keeping all your options in mind when you are doing these reviews.

Their dependence on you can also become a great exit strategy. Businesses that bring a new technology to the market and build their relationships with the local elite, often find them making large offers for their businesses. On the other hand, if this does become an exit strategy, one thing to keep in mind is that if you have too many deep relationships with partners, especially joint ventures, each of them may attempt to block to your exit.

---

[5] An OEM is a company that has a special relationship with computer and IT producers to resell the producers' product under their own name and branding.

5. *Believing One Country's Government Works the Same as the Other*

Even in Asia, each country works very differently. Many countries in Asia cannot even claim that their government functions in the same basic ways it did 10 or 20 years ago. Look at how Hong Kong has evolved since they moved from British to Chinese rule. Consider the changes we discussed in India's power structure and how they have changed. When looking at Southeast Asian governments and how they work with businesses, you'll find literally hundreds of major changes throughout Asia made during the last 20 years.

On the other hand, it's important not to group Asia into one large cluster, just as you wouldn't group North America into one large group. For example, business with the government is done very differently in Canada, the United States, and Mexico, let alone smaller countries in North America.

What then can you do to understand the differences between countries, especially subtle differences, like the difference in laws and government intervention between Hong Kong and Taiwan, both semi-Chinese territories? Expatriate support and your own research cannot speak accurately about how the government works in your sector. Don't despair. You can get a better understanding from your in-country support, who will have been working in your sector for years.

Keep an eye on how to work within the framework of these countries. At first glance, one might assume that a U.S. business cannot work in India because corruption is so rampant. But we are all aware of numerous U.S. firms actively working, and apparently succeeding, in India. There are methods, tried and true, to success in these countries; modeling after someone who did it before you is a good way to get your foot in the market. Finding out how to do it better than the people who went before you is the key to being great in the market. This can be done in a few ways, the easiest of which is modeling several successful businesses and taking from them their most successful practices. Another way to protect and grow your business is to take advantage of the actions of these large governments or powerful groups, either trying to move quickly where they are slow, or better yet, having them push you into markets they cannot or will not advance into.

CHAPTER 6

Building Your Strategy: How to Determine Where You Want to Go

Most people do not know the difference between a strategy and a plan. Strategy is your overlying idea of where you want to go; think of a ship captain saying we want to be at this port on Tuesday, this one on Friday, and another two weeks from now. The plan is how the captain will get to those locations; we will take this path with stops here and here, and go at this speed, and then it's up to the crew to execute this plan.

T he first step for us when we are working with a client—and we recommend it to any business—is to always develop a strategy, typically for market entry into one or two markets; occasionally, we do this for the company as a whole. *Ideally*, I think we should do this for a company as a whole *first*. If you do not know where the whole ship is going, how can you possible know where a part of it is going? Assuming you have a strategy for the whole of your business and now need one for your specific growth into Asia, let's consider several options:

- Do you need to be in one specific country? This happens often when a client is pushing you to be in the market.

- Do you want to explore several markets to find the best one for you? This is a good approach if you are not sure where your best growth opportunities are.

- How will you manage this? Is there an overlying strategy for Asia or is it country-specific? Do you have an Asian management team or do you have your area managers reporting up through their proper channels; for example, does your Asian finance director report to a corporate finance director? You probably need a blended approach to give your Asian managing director (or whatever you decide to call your senior manager in Asia) enough autonomy to run the business and make decisions while also making sure they are not completely segregated from the rest of the business.

Your strategy work should be clearly defined. Often, when we work with clients, they confuse strategy and planning. For us, forming a strategy involves the answers to a lot of questions: who you are, where you are coming from, where you are going, where the market is now, and where the market is going. Once we have gathered all of this information, we start to figure out appropriate goals for our clients.

Using these newly established goals and the information we have gathered on the company and the market, we consider how they will play in the market, what type of approaches will work for them, and why they will work for them. We analyze their supply chain to see how we can optimize the approaches we put in place and to figure out how all of these things play together. We also analyze areas where pitfalls—both internal and external—may arise. We frequently do a deep dive into the leadership challenges that may arise, which can be touchy—sometimes you have to tell your client why they are a problem for their own growth. If the company is honest with themselves, they may agree, but this conversation does not always lead to a happy response. Nevertheless, it's something every business leader should consider before making such a move.

In 2015, we took on a new client, X-IO Technologies. X-IO Technologies possessed premium technology for Intelligent Storage Elements (typically enterprise servers). In addition to this superior technology, X-IO tended to come in at a cheaper price than its competitors. They had previously done some work in China, and had outsourced a two-man sales staff from a company out of Hong Kong; the operation was running fairly efficiently considering only two people were tasked with all of China. The two employees were maxed out as far as head-quarters could tell. Complicating the situation was a transition at the top: Bill Miller had been brought in as chief executive officer (CEO) in February 2015. He, in turn, filled many positions throughout the company, including the vice president of international operations, Tim Cullen. In his new position, Tim had to figure out how to handle all of their international operations and needed help reviewing his staff and building a strategy for growth; he was not brought in to keep the status quo. After meeting with the staff in China, reviewing the employees and what they had to offer to X-IO, we were hired to build a growth strategy for the market. During this time, we reviewed the strengths and weaknesses that X-IO had in general, focusing on what made them unique. In addition, we reviewed what opportunities were out there, looking for low-hanging fruit as well as long-term possibilities.

Five Issues Many Companies Face When Developing a Strategy for Asia

Keeping X-IO's story in mind, I will walk you through challenges businesses confront and the work that we did for them.

I'll also examine markets that might play better for the issue at hand.

1. *Just Because It Is Legal to Sell in a Country Does Not Mean You Can (at Least Not Easily)*

To begin, review your markets for ongoing approvals and how the in-country market is handling things.

With X-IO, we were aware that they would be allowed to sell their products; they had been doing so for several years. However, recently, the Chinese government had been pressured into working exclusively with Chinese storage companies. As I mentioned earlier, an Ex-IOE approach was adopted, requiring government offices and state-backed operations to show just cause when using IBM, Oracle, and EMC (IOE) hardware and software. This directly blocked many top U.S. firms in the industry and also gave rise to Chinese companies that were able to secure the open contracts on the market. IBM, Oracle, and EMC adapted and refocused their efforts on the markets they could still pursue but also began to pursue OEM arrangements with Chinese companies that didn't yet have the necessary technology to compete.

What did this mean for X-IO? It meant a few things. First, in China, it meant that, like their Chinese competitors, X-IO had new potential clients to pursue. It also meant that they had rising Chinese competition to fend off. In addition, it meant that there was increasing rivalry in surrounding markets, as IBM, Oracle, and EMC now had more money to pursue new clients in other Asian markets, all while not ceding the Chinese market.

As a growing company, X-IO needed to focus on immediate victory for growth and could not afford to fight these large companies across all fronts. We put together a strategy that captured this and allowed X-IO to focus on the best potential growth sectors in China, shift from a push to a pull approach, and make many small changes that opened up opportunities that had not been seen previously.

2. *Consumers Do Not React in the Same Way in All Markets*
I often hear people talk about the rise of the Chinese middle class (for that matter, *I* often talk about the rise of the middle class in China)—a true phenomenon. However, "middle class in China" has a different meaning than it does in the United States. In general, the difference is about $12,000 per capita income in China and about $50,000 per capita income in the United States. Talk about a difference in purchase power. However, do not totally discount the Chinese consumer, because there are large differences in their tax situations, as well as other benefits, such as subsidized housing. If your strategy requires a higher-spending middle class for your products, take a look at other markets such as Japan, Hong Kong, or Singapore. These economies are wealthier on a GDP or per capita basis and, with this in mind, can put certain products to better use.

A question to ask yourself is "How does the market classify purchasing power?" Sometimes it's easier for people in the United States to think about Western Europe when analyzing areas like purchasing power because there are more similarities in countries like Great Britain, France, and Germany. Even when purchasing power levels out, how that money is spent varies greatly among countries. Many Asian countries have much higher savings rates than we do in the United States, although generationally this seems to be changing in these countries. As savings rates decrease, obviously spending rates increase. How does this affect your business and your strategy? If you're selling big-ticket items, such as a car, this could actually be a negative. Similarly, how does the country feel about borrowing? If borrowing is commonplace, how does that factor into your business? Can you finance your products for your customers or do you need a banking relationship to do that? Even if you can finance the products, do you want to?

3. *Your Message in One Country (Merely Translated) Can Fail in Another*
It's important to know your value proposition, a simple statement. However, you also have to know your value statement

in a new market. Most people assume it is the same, but look at X-IO Technologies. Their value proposition in the United States is that they have superior technology at a lower price than their competition. But in most Asian countries, low price is assumed to mean low quality and can distinctly hurt your sales. X-IO is better off with a value proposition of offering imported superior technology from an innovative market. A change like this in your "sales pitch" may be difficult for those inside your headquarters to understand, but on the street, when dealing with a client, your sales team better learn this quickly. (When a consultant recommends that a client raise its price in a new market and you pair that with a statement such as "this will increase your units sold," it's usually unexpected and can be met with skepticism. After all, we have all seen a simple supply-and-demand diagram.)

Most people have heard the famous story of the Chevy Nova, a car that sold remarkably well in the United States, only to flop in Latin American markets. Why? Because "no va" in Spanish roughly translates to "no go." Not exactly what you are looking for in the sales pitch for a car. Make sure you don't make this mistake. It seems like commonsense, especially when we have the ability to hire and communicate with staff in the country as easily as we can today, but these mistakes happen time and again around the world.

Where do you find the right messaging information? Do you go to high-end international marketing and branding firms? Do you go to local marketing and branding firms in your new markets? Can you do this internally? Some combination of all of these is needed to find the right messaging. Perhaps an international marketing and branding firm isn't necessary, but that depends on whether you are looking for uniform messaging across several markets. Did you know that a blonde woman is not considered desirable in certain markets like Burma? You must be careful even when choosing the hair color of the people in your print material. Ideally, you want someone that looks like your client; it's easier for people to see themselves using the product or service that way. But, in what markets can you simply replace the person and the text, and keep the rest of the layout the same. There have been campaigns from companies where this has been successful.

4. *Just Because the Competition Is in a Country Doesn't Mean You Should Be*

The reverse is also true: You should not just cede a market to a competitor. A proper review of the market will help tell you whether there is good opportunity for you. You should review the immediate market and compare it to similar markets to help make your best decision. In some sectors, you will find you need to be in the market when your competitor enters, such as Coke and Pepsi, where allowing the other to operate for any period of time on their own would mean ceding the market for the future. In others, your research may show that the market will not be profitable for you or your competitor, and you should avoid it.

Make an honest assessment of the markets, and if you struggle with being honest about your own company, do the assessment for your competitor. Oftentimes, we overestimate our own capabilities and claim we will hit goals in unrealistically short periods of time and/or in higher than expected amounts. As an outsider, is it sensible to assume you will hit profitability in six months, or take 75 percent market share? Perhaps, but unlikely. So, while it is not always easy to judge a market for your business, it can sometimes be easier to judge it for your competitors. It is often obvious to us what our competitor's weaknesses, as well as their strengths are. I hope this exercise helps as you review your own business. Look at the variances between your ability and your competitor's ability to achieve results in the market. Go back and assess the true differences in your abilities; more than likely, you will be correcting your numbers, not theirs.

This may be a good time to bring in an outside analyst to do an open and honest assessment of your business.

It is also important not to go into a market just because you like it. It seems simple enough: You shouldn't set up operations in Hawaii just because you like the beaches. Yet, sometimes people enter Japan because they're fascinated by the culture. What you do not know about your competitors is whether they entered a market for no better reason than that. When you are considering market entry, remember: The fact that you do your due diligence does not mean they do. So, when you are considering chasing them into a market, it's important to keep this in mind and not compete just to compete.

When the business case justifies it, it's time to ratchet up the offensive. Be prepared to compete and, if you are following a competitor into the market, remember that they have the upper hand. Figuring out a way to take this from them can be very difficult and very costly. You have to build and take relationships; you have to operate on their radar. They did not have to operate on yours. It's with this in mind that you must really consider how quickly to react when you see a competitor entering a market. Obviously, the less time they have to play in the market by themselves, the less ground you need to make up and the fewer relationships need to be captured for your company to succeed.

5.   *The Need to Change Your Strategy in Each Country*
It's important to remember that your strategy must change in each and every culture. If you are in the United States, would you sell your product the same way to a New Yorker as you would to a Texan or a Californian? Perhaps. But, you want to be sure before you take the same approach. Timing plays into this as well. Would a tech company sell their products in the same way in 1999 versus 2002? No. Events have occurred during those three years that tell them they must adjust as well, assuming they still exist.

Similarly, just because you have a competitor in your current market, this doesn't make them a competitor in the new market (does every gas station in the United States operate in every state?). Even if your competitor is in the new market, they may not be a competitor to you. For example, they may only sell a certain subset of products in a new market, or they may only operate in certain parts of a country. If a competitor in the United States goes into China and they operate in Shenzhen, and you decide to set up operations in Beijing, are you competing? Maybe, but more than likely you are not competing any more than if they had gone into Thailand and you went into Malaysia. Only research can tell you for sure.

This often holds true in China and India, which are huge markets, but it may be less true when operating in smaller Asian markets like Hong Kong, Singapore, or Taiwan. However, when looking through your markets, make sure that you consider each one as unique. Look at your product or service through the eyes of a local consumer. Try to understand how that product or service gets to the end user, and why it gets to them the way it does. If you cannot picture this because you don't have enough experience, go ask. In-country, go ask the specific buyer, or if you need more immediate answers, go poll college students from the country. We use Chinese interns all the time. They and their families come from varied backgrounds. In addition, they often did their undergraduate education with students who stayed in-country whom they can contact. With all of these immediate resources, we regularly get very quick answers about channels, pricing, and opportunities. We're able to pull together polled information almost overnight; we send it off before we leave the office and they return it while they are at work; it's in our email inbox the next morning. This may not be the way we would do it if we needed very specific or detailed information, but for general product information it's a good and cheap resource.

All of these information-gathering items still cannot tell you when to change your strategy. Obviously, if these things change and your sales forecast changes, it's a good time to change. Occasionally, businesses change their strategy because of "gut instinct." This is difficult to do if you're not really familiar with the market. Keeping your eyes wide open and your ear to the ground really can help in foreign markets. In a foreign market, relationships with U.S. Commercial Services and groups like the U.S. Chamber of Commerce can provide feedback from economists both in-country and from abroad about how the market in general is evolving, and also how your own sector is evolving, what regulatory changes may be coming, and what effect those changes might have on your sector.

Using the Ex-IOE policy example, if you know that is coming down the line, you might have decided to either pursue IBM's, Oracle's, or EMC's current clients to make sure that relationships were being built with them ahead of time, or you might have backed away from the market not knowing how the policy would play out on your own business. This is a great example of a time when information can be gathered, but a "gut instinct" may also be necessary.

When trying to optimize your Asian strategy, it's important to bring in people who understand several things. *First*, your business (ideally this is you); *second*, the Asian economies you are interested in (either in-house personnel or a consultant); and finally your business in that country (ideally, this person becomes your in-country manager). More often than not, this third piece gets left out until the end, but the in-country manager is extremely helpful when you're trying to understand the market dynamics and where pitfalls and opportunities may lie, and simply how to best run your business in a new market. These three people/groups will be able to tell you who you are, where you are coming from, and where you are going, and, then, how to get there, which we will tackle in our chapter on planning.

Often this strategizing to enter a new market comes as a piece of the organization's overall strategic planning. It's important to remember that building a growth strategy for the organization may tell you that you should enter the Asian markets because of opportunities that show up. This may be the major piece to your market entry strategy, but you'll need to go a little further and make sure you are identifying key market factors that will be deciding factors in your success to the market. The ideal scenario is for a company to develop their overall corporate strategy and then develop customized strategies for the new markets or products as needed, which will support a successful outcome in the overall strategy.

After answering all of the questions on where your product or service fits in the new market, what are some other key factors for strategy relating to Asia?

- The number one factor is people. Analyzing who you have and what you need. Can you develop a real focus on what you need in the market—not job titles, but what you are actually missing for understanding the market and eventually succeeding in it?

- The number two factor is time. You must understand the amount of time necessary to build your operations that will eventually lead to success. If you spent that same time further developing a current domestic strategy, which has greater value for the company? Short term? Long term?

- The third factor is total honesty and realism. Are you giving yourself too much credit and not being realistic about what your operations will do and the time necessary to do it?

All of these factors are important and all of them should be discussed when building a strategy for the organization.

CHAPTER 7

Designing Your Plan: What to Consider and How to Evaluate Them

Most really good companies are great at two things: building and executing a plan. They tend, though, to work a bit backward; first, becoming great at executing, and then building a plan around it. Seldom do they work top-down by building a strategy and then building their plan around a good strategy.

O ver the years, I've worked with some great economic development councils in cities throughout Asia. All of them operate a little bit differently, but in general they offer the same, or similar, thing: economic incentives to induce companies to set up their operations in their city. If you are not a *Fortune* 500 business or of significant size, this is a little less true insofar as major cities are concerned. Cities like Shanghai and Beijing, Tokyo, Singapore, and Hong Kong have less need to recruit small- or medium-sized businesses (I'm not saying they won't, just that it's less likely and less of a priority for them). Meanwhile, the governments in cities like Changzhou or Nanjing are eager to help you set up and grow. These cities are not just there with economic incentives; they show up with introductions to potential clients and potential suppliers and a true desire to see you succeed. Figure out what your needs are when you build your plan, not just what's easiest.

One thing I find particularly interesting about deciding where in Asia to set up a business—and it's fairly unique when compared with the rest of the world (with the possible exception of Europe, although not on the scale of Asia)—is that you need to figure out if you should choose a large, established market (Japan and China); a large, unestablished market (Indonesia); a small, established market (Singapore), or even a small, unestablished market (Malaysia, among many others). If you look at opportunities having established your categories and size, you then need to identify what type of country will work for you and your products or services.

Planning should encompass everything, from resources to timelines to targets; I look at it as a story to success, and liken it to the *Choose Your Own Adventure* children's books from the 1980s. You've come to this part in the process (your "story"), do you:

- Hire a local employee? ("If so, jump to page 35").

- Send in a current employee? ("If so, jump to page 72").

- Hire a consultant? ("If so, jump to page 20").

You may well ask, "Why do I need all of these resources to build a plan?" It's typical for a company to ask this question. We often think planning and strategy are very similar, and thus do not feel that we need a large team to build a plan, but the reality is planning needs to pull in more internal resources. Two common occurrences that can derail the train are 1) staff who are too busy with their other work to dedicate much time to the plan and so they either participate on a limited basis or send a junior person to participate in planning meetings, and 2) staff that simply doesn't want to participate, period.

> ➤ *The takeaway:* It's critical that you find support for the work currently on the planning team's plate, so your senior staff can fully participate and you can get their input where necessary.

Lack of buy-in will kill even the best laid plans, so getting your entire team onboard from day one is vital to the success of your project. If you do not have buy-in early on, you need to figure out the cause immediately and fix it. Finding a way to make senior staff be a part of the solution instead of the problem is a key in this scenario.

One more thing: There comes a point in the planning process when you'll need to start engaging an in-country team. This is hard, especially on smaller businesses, because it's a direct cost and you're not going to be generating revenues for several months, if you're lucky, and potentially, not for a year, or years, if you're not. You need an in-country team to develop the strategy for the same reason you need your senior "home" team to participate. If you bring in an in-country manager or Asian manager after the fact, someone can always say it wasn't their plan and that's why it failed.

> ➤ *The takeaway:* Giving managers the ownership necessary to call it their own plan, even though they were just a piece of it, is essential to the success of the operation.

Four Issues Businesses Encounter When Building a Plan

Your plan is your guide to success, but it must be fluid so you can modify it as you learn more and more each day. Your plan represents your guiding principles; it flows down from your strategy and should follow the strategy even as you change the tactics you employ.

1. *Location, Location, Location*

We have all heard it, usually as it pertains to real estate or restaurants, but where you set up in Asia matters immensely. How do you know if you are in the right location? Even if you know you're in the right country, how do you know if you're in the right city? It's a tough question to answer, but here's some advice:

- *Do not fall in love with a specific country because every-one else is going there or because you love to travel there.* If all your competitors are going there, that does not mean it's the right market for your business. However, it's probably worth paying attention to and review-ing to see if it is. Contrariwise, you cannot give away a market and leave it to a competitor if it's profitable, because their newfound money that you let them have will allow them to compete better in your home mar-ket. Likewise, if you are in love with a country because of the beauty or the culture, you should travel there for pleasure, not business.

- *Look for opportunities that align to your business inter-ests.* Review multiple countries and make sure you review them using the same criteria so that you can make an unbiased decision. Sometimes I hear business-people say that the two markets they're considering are different and should not be compared in the same way. But in my view, your inputs are the same, your time and your resources and, hopefully, the outputs are the same, profits not losses. Identify the best way to evaluate all of the factors and try not to skew a result to favor the coun-try you emotionally prefer; this is harder than it sounds as we do a lot of this unconsciously. If there's a trusted third party who understands your business and your company, ask that person to review the criteria you've used to ensure you have considered everything and your evaluation is fair.

For example, if you're looking at two markets, say India and China, the size of the country is a negligible consideration as they are both massive, but, let's say, in your heart you prefer India. You may skew the comparison and tell yourself, "We're looking at a country that is expected to grow infrastructure substantially over the next 10 years," leading you to select India because China has already built out extensively over the past two decades. What the statement may lead you to ignore is that your product needs established infrastructure in which to operate, so while building infrastructure is a key, previously established infrastructure may be even better because it will produce more immediate gains.

Typically when I do a city comparison for clients, I like to compare cities in the United States to foreign cities. It's easier for them to understand that they are making a decision between the New York City and the San Francisco of a foreign market than the Shanghai and the Shenzhen of a foreign market. This doesn't account for everything, but can give someone a basic understanding of the foreign markets and help them choose a city or two that they can then explore in depth. It'd be nearly impossible (or at least extremely costly) to give a client a true in-depth review of every city in Southeast Asia in order for them to make a decision. Breaking down cities and opportunities within each country and offering a few choices makes it easier for a client to review and make decisions. If you were to look at every city in China with more than one million people, you would have to review nearly 150 cities; how could you remember the difference among Nantong and Baotou and Changzhou? For this reason, when making a final decision, you should speak with the local economic development councils to find out what initiatives they are pushing forward and how they can support your personal business growth; you cannot do this with a large number of cities, but three or four is manageable, and you should do it.

> ➤ *The takeaway:* Select your top three or four cities; put
> boots on the ground and visit each city; meet with the
> economic development councils, potential partners,
> suppliers, and others. Seeing your growth opportunities
> up close is a must.

2.   *The High Cost of Doing It Right*

With a background in accounting and finance, this is a bit
painful to say, but most of the time you cannot nickel and dime
your way to success. It's going to be very costly to grow these
operations, and you'll need a lot of resources at your disposal
to cover operating costs, such as consultants, new employees
(both in your corporate offices and on the ground in the new
market), flights, hotels, temporary offices, and so on.

As noted previously, Asia is a relationship-based culture,
so you will need to "buy" these relationships by hiring the
right people—those who already have them—and developing
these relationships by spending time on the ground in Asia.
There's no substitute for either of these and more than likely
you'll need to do both. One without the other can still lead to
success, but it often comes at the cost of time, and no matter who you are, time is your enemy. If you take too long,
in-country businesses may scale up to compete with you, or
out-of-country businesses who acquired branding depth in the
interim may be able to move in because you opted to grow
slowly to save some short-term cash.

Most often companies tighten spending in areas they
should not, that is, people—both in-country representatives
and consultants. Even I have done this. Several years ago, a
company I worked for was growing their business presence
in China and we chose to send in someone from our staff,
rather than hiring from within the country, primarily because
we already had this person on staff and it was cheaper and
easier to send him. In addition, we felt we could do it on our
own, hiring the right legal and accounting teams in China, but
again we went for the least expensive option, and we ended

up spending a lot of time, effort, and money cleaning up after the accounting team we hired. Had we focused more on the long term instead of the short term, we would have seen these errors ahead of time, but it's easy not to see the forest for the trees, especially in economies that take a lot of time to go through all of the procedural steps.

There is, however, a time to be penny-wise, and that means not being wasteful. There are some really good local law firms and accounting firms in Asia; when they partner with your corporate lawyers or accounting firms, they can deliver the results you require. To give you some perspective, when our company first entered China, our law firm, Gallagher & Associates, charged roughly $2,000 per year to get us set up, manage registrations, and review all contracts for clients, vendors, and employees. Think about what that would cost in the United States if you were setting up in New York City (we were in Shanghai, which I compare to New York City). Keep in mind that the registration process takes months in China, not minutes like it does in the United States. Being conscious of your costs is a definite requirement if you are going to build something that does not hemorrhage money from day one.

And remember, it's essential that you negotiate all of these agreements with your vendors and partners because it's essential that you establish that you will not be a "sucker" who overpays for everything.

3.   *Whether or Not to Establish a Joint Venture*
On day one, a joint venture with an Asian company may make things easier. You have someone (ideally) that knows the local market, has relationships to sales channels, and eliminates some of the legwork involved in the initial setup. In addition, if your partner is the majority owner of the joint venture, you'll more than likely be seen as a local company and have opportunities to work with the government and other businesses when a local company is preferred.

Where a joint venture could potentially derail is after day one. We will examine this issue much more in depth in chapter 12, but it's worth noting here some of the things that need to be considered in the planning stage. If you're considering a joint venture, you need to:

- Take into account your partner's opening interest as well as their end game. Are they content with dominating their local market or do they want Asian or international expansion? How does that play into your own thoughts on the joint venture?

- Consider what you're gaining from the joint venture. Do you intend to joint venture on a product or product line, but not your entire business, so that you can learn enough to take other products into the market in the future?

- Think about what happens when, eventually, your joint venture winds down. Will you be able to run your own business moving forward in the market, if you have been hands off? More than likely you won't, so you need a plan to make sure you gain the knowledge and experience every day along the way. This obviously requires that your own team spend more time on the ground, which may in itself substantially reduce the joint venture's usefulness to you.

4.   *The Need to Update and Adjust Their Plan*

Especially if you're in smaller, more transitional markets, your plan will require frequent tinkering. An easy way to think about this is to ask yourself if you were in China 20 years ago whether your plans have remained the same throughout the last two decades. No, you'd have constantly adjusted them as the market adjusted. If you were a products-based business, you'd have started out with brick and mortar stores, and when Alibaba entered the picture, you'd have adjusted to selling more and more online. This holds true throughout Asia. If you're looking at market growth in Vietnam today, you should evaluate the likelihood of the Trans Pacific Partnership (TPP) being passed and whether it will have an effect on how you're going to do business tomorrow. You should put some plans in place based upon market assumptions, but you also need to know that these plans will change almost daily in the coming years as new information comes to light and new opportunities open up. You cannot think of this as Asian NAFTA and assume you know what will happen moving forward. For that matter, even if you're looking at countries that are not part of the TPP, but are in Asia, you'll need to understand how TPP may impact your business.

The old adage "the best laid plans . . ." is even more true in evolving and volatile climates. Knowing when to adjust and when not to adjust is the key. As a government changes (or perhaps is overthrown, as it has been several times in Thailand), how does that affect your business? Do you need to adjust your plans or can you stay the course? It's very common that we believe we need to change during these times, but doing so wouldn't always be correct. Some changes affect certain companies, and not others.

Look at China and all that has happened under President Xi Jinping. The driving factor for China under President Xi has been to become the number one economy in the world and to be recognized as such. To do this, one of the many changes that were seen as necessary was the elimination of the rampant corruption throughout the country. As a result, many, many people have been imprisoned and some executed. So, let's say you were an American company operating in China when President Xi came into office (and operating in compliance with the FCPA), would you have known on day one how much this would affect your competition and how you'd be able to accelerate your growth simply by continuing to operate as you were because several government employees needed to very quickly find relationships that were uncontroversial and some companies were better able to quickly take on new clients than others?

On the other hand, during the same period, we saw the Ex-IOE policy put into effect in China. Those three dominant companies, IBM, Oracle, and EMC, will have to make huge changes to their plans for their China operations. However, if you're a smaller U.S. or European company that competes with these three, there may be a massive opportunity that you can adjust your plans to capitalize on.

Building a plan is an essential element to your success. Hopefully, I have demonstrated the imperative in being able to fine-tune your plan as changes occur in the marketplace. Most of the Asian countries you explore will not have the benefit of the stability of the U.S. government. Conversely, depending on how you view them, some may offer more stability. For instance, it will not take them nearly as long to change or implement laws; things do not take years as they do in the United States where congressional and executive (and sometimes judicial) approval is required.

Design your plan with the mind-set that you are setting up a new business and building a business plan. Cover the necessary topics to set up a completely new business, because effectively what you are is an informed, and, ideally, well-capitalized new business in a foreign market. Taking the time to realize this and work through it ahead of time will save you countless hours later on. Important reminder: Do not overlook how this might affect your other business lines.

Ronnie Chan, chairman of Hang Lung Properties and Hang Lung Group (owners of many high-end malls in China, as well as numerous other properties and international businesses), when discussing the high-end stores in his malls and other malls throughout China, very thoughtfully noted that some of the stores pay close to no rent; they're used to attract other tenants—after all, who would not want to be located next to the Cartier store? In addition, the goals, in Chan's view, of these high-end stores was not to set sales records—customer traffic is light for them; instead, their goal was to break-even and generate enough buzz so that when the Chinese nationals traveled to Hong Kong or New York or London, they made purchases at these stores during their travels. Effectively, the strategy and plan for these stores in China was marketing—quite expensive marketing if you think about the overhead required to run the store—but, obviously, feasible since companies continue to operate in this manner.

Why is a plan so essential? Taking a strategy and simply telling someone to execute on your strategy leaves too much room for interpretation and means you are putting your faith in one or two people as opposed to building upon a team effort. Utilizing all of your experience is crucial when building your initial plan. This does not need to be a long process. We have done it in one month, and we have done it in over six months, but it has some essential characteristics that need to be satisfied, and as long as you can meet them, you can move forward knowing that you've developed a thoughtful plan to enter the market.

CHAPTER 8

Executing Your Strategy and Plan: The Implementation Phase

Execution is the name of the game. If you cannot execute, you cannot survive. In any situation, at home or abroad, manufacturing or services, internal or external, if you cannot get it done, there'll be no tomorrow.

O nce you've developed your strategy and the plans to execute it, it's time to put on your boots and walk through the mud. It's not going to be easy and it is what separates the winners from the losers. You're going to need additional staff, but hopefully you're transitioning from overhead to billable resources, maybe not right now, but soon.

If yours is like most companies who have come this far, here's a bit of what you might expect:

1. As you begin to execute and set up your operations, you walk through your supply chain, find issues with it, develop better options, and adjust as necessary.

2. In addition, you build out your own internal competencies and improve your own operations.

3. You also begin to develop sales strategies and relationships. This is probably the first time in your process when the light bulb goes on and you realize why someone suggested one way of doing this and not another, where theory moves to action, and you start to see the product of your hard work. In some ways, this is the most fun; it can also be the most exhausting part of the process.

It's important not to be shortsighted here. It's easy to get caught up in one piece of the operation and let other opportunities slide. One of the saddest things I see is a company manufacturing in China and not selling there. The same holds true throughout Asia. Cheap labor has been chased for years and will continue to be chased far into the future. Some companies are exceptionally good at building operations around reduced costs. I understand chasing cheap labor and lower manufacturing costs, but I do not understand not selling when opportunity presents itself.

Over the past 20 years, Chinese labor has become increasingly expensive. In fact, I rarely recommend companies manufacture in China anymore with one big exception to this rule: that is, *unless* you want to sell in the Chinese markets. If you can gain market share, reduce tariffs, or reduce transportation costs that can provide you with an advantage in the market, it can still make sense. Why would anyone want to go to all the effort of setting up a business entity with only half the gain? Keep this in mind wherever you set up operations throughout Asia. Utilize your manufacturing platform to expand sales. If you're going to attempt to maximize efficiency, then you shouldn't do it halfway.

Managing Your Supply Chain

Manufacturing in Asia can be a great opportunity and a large piece to your supply chain. However, even if you're not thinking of manufacturing there, you need to consider the changes in your supply chain that'll occur as you enter the Asian markets. More than likely you're not going to ship straight from the United States or Europe unless you can sell your product at a premium in the market with a "Made in United States" or "Made in Europe" label on it. Selling some products at an up-charge is feasible in certain categories; for example, items such as medical devices, information technology, and legal services sell at a higher price if made in the United States or Europe (or, in the case of services, are bolstered by a U.S. or European brand) because Asians believe that the quality is needed in the particular product category. As you develop your strategy and planning, you'll need to figure out if this applies to your products or services.

For the sake of simplicity, let us assume your supply chain will change in Asia, either because the product is slightly different or because you need to make your supply chain more efficient to compete with market pricing. Keep in mind that companies like FedEx and UPS aren't prevalent in Asia, so very standardized ways of shipping things are not readily available. There are other options. If the desired destination is in the same city, bike or scooter messengers are everywhere, but they can only handle small batches or small products. If you're moving larger items, you may have to design your own supply chain logistics.

Sourcing is also an issue. With many products restricted or not native to Asia, you need to determine how you'll source materials. Are you able to maintain quality control on your products, especially if you're sourcing them from several different areas or companies? If you are not building a lot of products in Asia, just supplementing, options such as Alibaba may work to source parts and supplies, but as you grow your operations you'll need better options. This is a case where working with the government, both in the United States (or Europe) and the Asian country you're doing business in, will pay dividends as they offer introductions, background checks, and resources that can be trusted (especially when you're using both your local government and the Asian government to vet companies).

We have seen clients and others run into several issues such as suppliers showing them a facility they didn't own to give the impression of a much higher-quality factory than they actually operated. More common is providing an inferior product. This is generally done, as previously discussed, by testing your tolerance by incrementally reducing the quality over time; meaning the first batch shipped may be top quality, the second batch shipped at 50 percent of this quality, and, if you don't question this, the third batch is at 50 percent of the quality of the second batch, and so on. It's up to you to catch this and call the supplier on it right away to make sure that the value of your own products is not degraded. This is also true if you only outsource production and sell into the United States or Europe.

There are some great examples of operational and supply chain efficiency in Asia—for example, Li & Fung, a global supply chain manager who specializes in clothing and derives its value from supply chain optimization. There are others like Li & Fung who specialize in other sectors; but Li & Fung is the most well-known and probably the largest supplier. This global supply chain manager has a lot of great qualities, such as the ability to batch orders and shift manufacturers where there is open capacity for a quicker turnaround. Its capabilities and its commitment to quality, safety, and compliance are truly valuable when you are looking to source materials and build a supply chain. In addition, Li & Fung offers many cost-saving opportunities by batch processing, mixing client's orders into large containers instead of shipping small batches, and overseeing vendors. Regarding other operations, look to see their experience in your industry, how much have they done, where have they done it, and whether it has created an advantage for a competitor. Answering these questions can give you valuable insight into how your own operation may benefit or whether you should seek someone else.

Five Execution Errors Businesses Tend to Make

There's no one single key to successfully executing in Asia. Perhaps the best advice that I can give is do not expect it to be like it is at home. In fact, expect everything to be different. Not exactly specific advice, but what you'll find is that it's very different and you need to be flexible and know when to push and when to give. This is why I have stressed the importance of having in-country staff. They will know when to give. What you'll have to assess is whether they know when to push and whether they'll tell you when you need to push. In some Asian cultures, people defer to the senior person or team, meaning they'll say they agree with you, even when they do not.

1. *Assuming Everything in Asia Is Done as It Is in the United States*
It's important to understand that someone in the United States who excels at executing your planning may not be able to do the same thing in a foreign country. For example, let's say your accounting team runs like clockwork in the United States, handles your process from front to back, and doesn't miss a beat. However, accounting practices are different in Asia than they are in the United States. Asia doesn't follow Generally Accepted Accounting Principles (GAAP); instead they use International Financial Reporting Standards (IFRS) accounting practices. In fact, this is true not only in Asia, but in most of the world.

> ➤ *The takeaway:* A situation like this is a great time to blend staff, to use both local and expatriate staff, to execute your planning. Utilizing in-country talent to better understand the local market and how it acts together with your own staff and business practices brings a best-practices approach to the market and allows you to optimize your operations.

Going back to the accounting example, to execute in this environment you need someone who understands IFRS accounting practices, but you do not want to ignore your knowledge and the benefits of GAAP. Finding someone to execute a blended approach will allow you to gain the knowledge necessary to operate in Asia without giving up too much. A friend of mine from Honeywell recently remarked that part of the reason they were killing it in China was their ability to bring in their best practices and implement them, whereas competitors in the market were still too fat to operate as quickly and efficiently as they were. He noted that they have also done a great job carrying over their hiring practices, which has allowed them to select the right talent in-country.

2.   *Sending an Expat to Do a Local's Job*
Sometimes it's good to send in someone who knows your operations, your sales strategies, and your product line, and so on from top-to-bottom. They know what makes your company your company. And sometimes, it is better to let a local do the legwork. We regularly work with Chinese firms coming to the United States, and we see how most of them approach establishing businesses in the United States. Often they send over a recent college graduate, buy them a car, and tell them to figure out their market setup. More recently, we've observed that they've been acquiring U.S. firms as a way to enter a market. However, more and more, we have been encouraging the middle ground, growing organically through greenfield projects, and hiring U.S. citizens with experience in the field. (In many disciplines, a "greenfield project" is one that lacks constraints imposed by prior work. The analogy is to that of construction on greenfield land where there is no need to work within the constraints of existing buildings or infrastructure.[1])

Why shouldn't U.S. firms take the same approach when entering Asian markets? If you look at this with unbiased

---

[1] https://en.wikipedia.org/wiki/Greenfield_project

eyes, you'll see that utilizing a local talent to make introductions, turn relationships into clients, and help you navigate through the local landscape makes a lot of sense in
foreign markets. After all, do you know the proper hiring
process in every Asian country? That's easy enough to figure out. Perhaps a better question is do you know the proper
firing process in every Asian country? Hiring a person in
Asia is easy, but firing them can be very difficult. In fact,
you'll typically find a joint venture partner trying to dump
their dead weight on you so that they don't have to termi-
nate employees.

3. *Expecting Business to Be Conducted on an American Timeline*

My first time in China, I thought I knew what I was doing.
I had set up a joint venture in Singapore, and the company I
worked for was hired by the Chinese government to come in
and design museums. We did nothing of sensitivity that might
be seen as controversial, that is, we were not defense con-
tractors, despite being high profile. We were being brought in
because we were a famous international design firm. I thought
I'd easily walk in, set up operations, and coast through the
registration process. Nine months later, I had my company
registered and could legally operate within China. At the time
I was irritated that it had taken so long, so many wasted days
going over and over the same basic items, changing a letter
here, a letter there, nothing of any significance. But it was
required. As I grew more and more angry over the delays,
I got notes from our law firm and our accounting firm con-
gratulating me on getting the office set up so quickly. I was
astounded. I felt nothing but anger over how long it took to
set things up. Yet, later, I found out that at the time it typically
took foreign firms 12+ months to get set up, if they were able
to register a Wholly Owned Foreign Enterprise (WOFE) at
all. At the time, WOFEs were heavily restricted and it was
difficult at best to get them registered.

My point is that you cannot expect the same timeline as it'd take to set up a business in the United States. There are countries that you can get registered in a lot easier than China. Singapore has a fairly simple setup, and in Hong Kong it takes about 45 days to get registered and be up and operating. Japan has a more extensive process, but, in the end, the government will work with you to get you up and running.

> *The takeaway:* Know what you are getting into from a time standpoint so that you don't blame your team for situations out of their control.

4. *Lacking Cultural Sensitivity*

Remember the cultures are different, and things that may go unspoken in the United States or Europe may be asked or stated in Asia. When I first set up operations in China, I was commuted back and forth; we were vetting partners that could fabricate exhibits for us in China, and I was speaking to several firms at the same time. Obviously, if you're a company trying to win the partnership of a renowned international firm that's being brought in to design major exhibits in your home country, and you want to do the fabrication for them, you'll be on your best behavior.

As the chief financial officer of the international firm, I was flying in to meet with everyone because my title gave these companies the peace of mind that I could speak on behalf of the business, which in their eyes our in-country manager could not. One partner asked me how old I was. I was 27, and I'm sure this was on the minds of several people I worked with at that time. As I told her my age, her next question was, how can someone who is 27 be chief financial officer and make decisions for the business? This caught me off guard, and was more difficult to answer. I responded that in the United States we cared more about what someone was capable of producing than whether they were male or female, young or old, or any other demographic factor. I'm not sure she understood the concept, but it satisfied her sufficiently enough to move forward.

We have talked a lot about the formality of relationships in Asia and, as this story indicates, status meant a great deal then and still does. Particularly at the beginning of a relationship, you, your chief executive officer, chief financial officer, chief operating officer, and others on your senior staff who are involved—names and titles mean a lot in Asia—need to show up and be a part of proceedings. They need to have drinks, go to dinners, take meetings, and be a part of the show. This isn't a one-man act. Those are always awful in the theater, and they're just as awful in the office.

As you move forward with partnerships and sales opportunities, and as your operations grow in Asia, it's common for a senior team to let their in-country or Asian managers take over and run operations. What's important to remember is that as the senior leadership of the company, you'll need to return and show your presence. When I work with clients, I like to:

- *Arrange a speaking engagement for a high-level executive, CEO, COO, etc.* Speaking engagements are a good way, especially in Asia, to demonstrate the true leadership and credibility of the company. It also gives your in-country team a chance to invite clients or potential clients to watch the senior team speak and see the team without spending large amounts of time in individual meetings.

- *Meet with larger clients.* Make sure they get the face time they desire, so they do not move on to another vendor. Another way to do this is to invite them to your U.S. or European headquarters. Giving your clients an excuse to travel, especially abroad, is a great way to get face time with them without having to travel yourself, and it will give you one-on-one face time without distractions.

- *Meet with potential new clients.* These are the people who most want to see the senior team. It tells them that their business is important to your company. If you don't show up, someone else will. So be selective, use your in-country team to work with, and vet the opportunities that actually require the presence of the senior team, and that offer the value to make it worth your time and effort.

For any of these, you can easily spend more time in-flight than on the ground, so make sure it's worth your while. There are direct flights now from the United States into many countries in Asia, including Japan, China, Hong Kong, and others. However, there are still a lot of countries without direct flights. Singapore is a great example, but there is a lot of work happening there. I have flown to Singapore from Washington, DC, through Hong Kong, landing in Singapore at midnight so that I could sign documents in the morning with a new client, and flown home by midafternoon I was in Singapore for all of 15 hours—it took me about 55 hours of flight time to get there and back.

> *The takeaway:* Face time is essential, but before you go, make sure it's worth the flight time.

5. *Assuming an Expat Assignment in Asia Is Just Another Transfer*

I'm not talking about the employee going over. I think most people understand they're not in Kansas anymore. I'm referring to the company that's sending an employee to Asia. It's important for the company to remember how difficult this transition can be and find ways to help the employee still feel tied back in to their home. As employers, we tend to minimize the actual transition. An employee leaves and they come back home once or twice a year. In the meantime, holidays happen, and they're away from their family; illnesses happen, and they're forced to figure things out. Effectively, life happens.

These things all have an effect on the employee themselves, and it's vitally important that the company remember this.

When our design firm first set up our office in Singapore, we sent several employees over there; 10 years later, several of them are still there. I used to send candy over in care packages around the holidays, candy corn at Halloween, candy hearts for Valentine's Day, and jelly beans at Easter. It was my way of connecting them back to their home, even if they could not be there.

On the other hand, when illness strikes it's frightening. We sent one of our senior designers to Shanghai to work on a project for a few months. During that time, a client in Israel requested his help, so he flew to Tel Aviv for a week. Toward the end of the week, he developed pain in his abdomen, which grew worse day by day. The day prior to his return to China, he was admitted to the hospital and diagnosed with gallstones. He was hospitalized for several days. I can't tell you how relieved I was that it happened while he was in Israel and not in Shanghai; health care is much better in Israel.

You have to remember this when you send an employee abroad. I've failed to remember this at times, focusing purely on the bottom line, and I know from experience that it's essential to keep in mind that you're sending a person to live in a place where they have no connections, so plan accordingly and take necessary precautions.

People, People, People

A few things I'd like you to take away from this, and they relate more to people than anything else:

➢ Know when to outsource (to companies like Li & Fung).

➢ Know when to bring in an expat to do the work.

➢ Know when you need local talent to do the work and make the introductions.

The number one thing that you should take away from this chapter is that it comes down to the people you surround yourself with. After putting together a strong strategy and plan, it's the feet-on-the-street that builds success. It's up to you to know the type of people you need.

CHAPTER 9

What to Consider When Making the Go/No Go Decision

Whenever you see a successful business, someone once made a courageous decision.

~ Peter F. Drucker

After building a strategy for market growth, along with a plan to execute it, you must then decide whether you should move forward and which market(s) to move into. This can be a tough decision. You have plowed ahead and spent time and money, and, potentially, you could tell yourself that you should stop and stay focused on your current market. What are the most important factors that you, as an executive in charge of this project, should focus on to make your decision?

The decision may not be made by 10 people sitting around a table, like you see in *The Thomas Crown Affair* when Pierce Brosnan is selling and buying businesses with all his advisors and his counterpart's advisors at a conference room table, but it should be a formal decision. A company cannot run through this whole process without taking a deep breath before making a "go" or "no go" decision. Too often, companies say they made the decision when they began the process of writing a market entry strategy, which is a first step in the fix bad breaking process. That's not the point at which a company should decide to move forward. Designing a strategy *and* mapping a plan are integral parts of the process. They're there to help a company make the decision about whether or not to move forward, and until you do both, you should refrain from making that decision. So, keeping that movie theme in mind, neither should the decision be made by one person, à la *The Godfather* to continue with another movie analogy, leaving the rest of the company blindly following behind.

When making the decision, keep timelines, goals, and milestones in mind. Be ready to make the decision to change your strategy or plan or even pull out, but do not say, "We were not profitable in year one, so we should leave." Be realistic and prepared to change. By being prepared, you have the information you need to analyze the situation, but you should bear in mind that just as you know more on day one of entry than you did on day one of designing a strategy, you should know more as you move forward. So, while you may not update your strategy, plan, or goals every day, you should use them as reference and update them from time to time as you gather new information.

I have in the past made the mistake of letting this decision go and, effectively, turned the decision making over to our clients. This was a costly mistake. After being hired by the Chinese government, Gallagher moved full steam ahead to get set up. We didn't stop to design strategy and plans; we didn't make a formal decision; and we didn't analyze whether or not we could find a cheaper and easier way to do it. This was a mistake that I participated in making about 10 years ago and not one I would make today. My point is that we let "no decision" become a decision; we were blinded by the opportunity. I have learned a lot from my mistakes along the way. Don't let yourself make the same mistakes. As a consultant, I'm not the decision maker, but today, I continually warn my clients against allowing this to happen to them.

As Peter Drucker wrote, you have the opportunity to make a courageous decision. Often, people forget that not making a decision is a decision, too. If you spend months building a strategy and plan, only to say we'll revisit it in six months or a year, you've effectively made a decision to not enter a particular market at that particular time. These markets change, maybe not enough in six months to make a difference, but perhaps there will be a change. Can you say there was a difference in the U.S. market from May 2008 to November 2008? Most people would respond definitively, "Yes." By pushing a decision off to a later date, you may be saying that the market at present is not right, and instead of entering it you will start over when the time is better (one hopes with more information than you had before you began the process).

1. *Five Decision-Making Mistakes Companies Often Make Going Forward Because of the Sunk Cost Effect*

Companies frequently go through the process of developing a strategy and a plan and determining the costs to market entry. Then comes the grand decision: Should we actually go ahead and enter the market? It's a decision only you can make, and it can be difficult, not least because you have spent countless dollars and hours getting to this point. But those dollars and hours should not be part of your consideration. They are sunk costs that you cannot get back. So, if your business plan doesn't clearly define a path to success, you may need to decide moving forward isn't in the company's best interest, or, at the very least, not in its best interest today. If you're not ready to entirely give up on the idea, consider identifying the items that would have to change that'd indicate a better time to enter; for example, when cash flow can better support the initial losses or when certain suppliers enter the market and you can source from in-country. No matter what the issue is, if there are one or two factors that can drastically change your go/no go decision, monitor the market to determine the right timing.

I tell clients they need to make this decision themselves because, as a consultant, I have a bias toward moving forward. That doesn't stop me from telling them that it doesn't make financial sense for them to enter a market, but obviously, it might sway some consultants. Understand that everyone you're listening to has an inherent bias toward a decision. Some biases are personal. For example, does a top executive receive a larger bonus this year if a no go decision means higher corporate profits instead of making a go decision and spending for the future? Does your senior operations person hate traveling abroad, or does your top sales person love to travel to Asia? This doesn't mean that their decision is right or wrong; it means it's impossible for someone not to have a bias. It's up to you, as a group, to identify the biases that may come into play when making decisions like this.

Going beyond the initial decision, you may need to identify a time or situation where you would pull out of a market. Once again, do not let those sunk costs prevent you from making the right decision. As with a gambling addiction, staying in the game does not mean you will make back the money you have lost. If you do not see the trend changing, you must have the wherewithal to pull out of the market. This is often the hardest decision; you have committed yourself to it and saw potential when you went into it, but the situation has changed. Are you able to change your mind based upon what that market is telling you?

Following this same thought process, there may come a time where you have to pivot out of one country and into another. If you've not been there for long and haven't recouped your initial investment, it's important to make sure that you are making a wise business decision. A good example of this is China. Companies have flocked to China for years to capture cheap labor, but if your company was late to the game and only began manufacturing there in the late 2000s or early 2010s, you may not have benefitted in the way others who moved in earlier have. As labor rates continue to rise, your company will not gain benefits, so if your model is dependent on cheap labor, a move to Vietnam or Indonesia or a number of other countries may be in your best interest.

- *The takeaway:* Don't let yourself be discouraged because of an initial perceived failure; instead identify what you learned, determine what could be done better next time, and move forward in the best interest of the business.

2. *Choosing the Wrong Market*

When comparing markets, how do you decide which market you should enter? A tough decision, especially if you can only afford to move forward in one market at a time. Do you choose the market that offers the strongest long-term opportunity or the market that offers a path to immediate success? There's no one good answer to this question. There are a few good rules of thumb to keep in mind:

- *Do not automatically take the easy path.* Just because it's easiest does not make it the best path for your business in either the short or long term. Currently, it's very easy to set up operations in Singapore and some good markets where you can get fast penetration, but you'll be operating in a market that doesn't have tons of upside for growth because of the small size of the island. There are obviously multiple schools of thought about this issue. Josephine Angelini (author of *Star Crossed*) wrote, "So, what can't you take? Decide which of the two options is harder, and do the other. That way, no matter how hard your choice turns out to be, at least you can find comfort in knowing you're avoiding something even worse."

- *Do not let long-term promise sway you too much.* Potential is great; it's an amazing thing to point toward; but how long can you wait for potential to pan out—two years, three years, five years? My guess is not too many companies will allow you to look beyond five years of potential, and you'd need a very patient and understanding senior leadership (almost, undoubtedly, a privately held company that did not have to answer to shareholders) that would wait five years. Not achieving potential doesn't mean you experience losses of 100 percent during those initial years; however, what you should see are trends that show you growing closer to your potential over time.

- *Do not just follow the herd.* It'd be perfectly understandable if you focused more upon China or India in Southeast Asia than other countries. You could cite the growth in these markets, especially China's, in recent years or look to the population and perhaps the demographics of those markets. But frequently, someone tells me they're interested in a market because their competitors are there, or so many others are there, and that, clearly, they should be there, too. This may be a good reason to take a look at that market and build a market entry strategy, but it's not a reason to just move forward and do it.

- *Do not let upfront cost decide.* Large upfront costs are hard to ignore, but if there are large potential profits on the back end, they may be justified. Of course, if you don't have the funds to cover large upfront costs, that may make your decision for you.

- *If available cash is not the issue, pursue all projects with a positive net present value.* One of my finance professors at Washington University in St. Louis made this statement and, in theory, it is true: With no financial constraints, chase all projects that will provide a positive net present value. Moving beyond the theory of a professor, you're working with many unknowns and potential changes when put into practice. The simple answer is to provide a high enough discount rate to justify the risks in the market, but even this can be hard to quantify.

3. *Expecting Success to Come too Quickly.*

Do not make the mistake of not entering a market just because you won't turn a profit in year one or year two. Perhaps you can, but that's the exception to the rule. In years one and two, you can expect to see progress and, hopefully, decreasing losses that show you're moving towards profitability and growth. To be fair, in years one and two, you may see increasing losses as you grow to meet market demand in years three and four, but, hopefully, with success in sight. On the other hand, if you see unexpected growing losses, you may need to reevaluate your business plan to make sure it's still viable.

Sometimes the hardest decision to make is to pull out of the market. Understanding that your sunk costs are irretrievable is important, not just on day one, but also in the future. As a member of senior leadership, it's important not to overly chastise those who designed your strategy and planning or the people who executed it. By steering clear of a personal mistake conversation, you avoid unintentionally discouraging your employees from trying again on your next endeavor. Of course everyone needs to accept responsibility for the part they played; knowing how to make sure people know their own failures versus corporate failures can be a difficult process and has to be handled delicately. Many circumstances and developments are outside of the control of your team, and if the issues were identified early on in your strategy and planning, and you were aware of them and able to monitor the changes as they arose, you may experience fewer losses because you identified and monitored problems and pulled out of the market sooner rather than later.

When I was part of the Executive MBA program at Washington University in St. Louis, we visited China for class and were required to write a market entry strategy plan for a business of our choice. These were somewhat detailed plans; some were for businesses that actually existed, while others were businesses that were invented for the market potential the students saw on the trip. The ideas varied quite a bit, but one thing

I observed was a false belief in how fast people felt they could capitalize on the potential of a market. There were eight presentations, not including mine. Of those eight, all but one predicted profitability from day one. No one recognized the time it would take to set up the business and the costs associated with it; neither did they recognize the difficulties involved in operating in a foreign market and how hard it would be to gain traction. These were very smart people—people you would be fortunate to work for and with, but even they didn't recognize that immediate success would not happen.

With few exceptions, I tell companies to expect losses in years one and two; ideally from year three on, you can capture profits. Those first two years are about growth and come at a cost. This is very similar to most start-ups, but, in this case, it's a start-up in a foreign country. Whether you're a new or experienced business, I consider you a start-up in a new market.

4. *Following a Best-case Scenario*
What does your worst-case scenario tell you? You're better off following your worst-case scenario than your best-case scenario. It may be nearly impossible to hit those low marks, but if your worst-case scenario still says that you should move forward, you're in a good position. Moving forward under the worst-case scenario means that your boss or your board shouldn't expect the world and, if you're right, you will trip over the low bar you've set. Assuming you haven't overestimated your own capabilities by too much, you should be in good shape if you follow your worst-case scenario. worst-case scenarios usually revolve around setup, because planners expect timelines similar to those they experience at home.

Frequently, decision making comes down to what is written in the plan, as well it should. Therefore, make sure that you have not overestimated your own talent or put forth market conditions that can't last or, worse yet, do not exist. It'd be foolish to claim you'll take 20 percent market share on day one or to be set up in the market in one week. While it's always an issue when people overestimate their abilities or the firm's capabilities, it's a bigger issue when you are making decisions based on these errors and omissions.

- *The takeaway:* If your team decides to move forward using your best-case scenario, it's unlikely that your in-country team will ever hit those metrics. You have set them up for failure.

When I set up FDI Strategies, I was fortunate enough to draw on the experience and intelligence of Bill Miller when I was raising capital. Bill has had an amazing career: He co-founded StorageNetworks, Inc., and essentially created cloud storage. Since that time, Bill has successfully invested in several other major companies, started his own hedge fund and venture fund, and currently runs X-IO Technologies. To say he has significant experience is an understatement. When I raised funds and started the business, he continually coached me on the need to follow a worst-case scenario rather than what I saw as our company trajectory. It was not a case of confidence; it was about managing expectations, and when times got hard and we needed our investors' support, Bill's foresight and mentorship made those discussions possible.

5.   *Believing the Go/No Go Decision Is the Last Step*
There's an old saying that an idea is worth nothing; execution is where the money is. Building a strategic plan is extremely important. Without it, you cannot decide whether you should enter a market or which market to enter. However, the fun is just beginning; If you cannot execute on a plan, it's really not worth anything more than the paper it is written on. People often make the mistake of putting a plan in place and thinking that the task of making it work is someone else's problem. This is just not the case. For this reason, we encourage the whole senior team and the leaders of the in-country team to participate in the planning.

What you need to be most afraid of is that people check out. Obviously, the in-country team will play an integral role in the execution and decision making but the senior leaders in the United States or Europe need to maintain a role.

Something to consider is the type of organizational structure you will put in place for your in-country or in-region team. This is an important thing to consider. If you work off of a matrix structure, your in-country team will report—at least on the dotted line, if not fully—to their departmental leaders. Does that work in your home market and other markets? Working through this issue as part of your decision-making process is of the utmost importance when running your analysis.

Other questions to consider include:

- If you have a city manager in Shanghai or Beijing, does that manager have more authority than a country manager in Mongolia or Singapore?

- How will you gauge the size of the market, population, GDP, and estimated market potential, and what factors will you use to evaluate potential growth of the market?

These are all decisions that are typically made in the planning phase, but how they will actually play out does become an important decision when they are no longer theoretical.

Decision making is a team effort; it shouldn't be left to one person. If you make it a one-person decision, you will lose buy-in, and potentially set yourself up for failure. Obviously, someone in the organization has to have the ability to say "go" and "stop," if it's the wrong decision. But, that go/ no go decision has to be made based on the best interest of the organization as a whole.

While there's much to consider, the decision-making process should be fairly quick. It effectively is a "yes" or "no" decision, without a lot of grey area; that is, unless your process also includes other options, such as should you joint venture, should you do it alone, should you license your intellectual property. Even so, you should already have built a business case that was strong enough for you to make the decision. If you have not, then you're not ready to make a decision.

Typically, I find the hardest part of this is getting consensus and getting the vote of everyone who should be voting. Sometimes there are people who are afraid to go against what the boss has decided and do not voice their true opinions; at other times, there are people who are unsure, and therefore go along with the majority. Make sure you find out why they are unsure or what they really think, so that you can factor that into everyone's decision.

- *The takeaway:* Sunk costs aside, the cheapest decision you can make is not to enter the market; that doesn't make it the best decision, but remember that option when you're making your decisions.

CHAPTER 10

Joint Ventures and Franchising: The Pros and Cons

The fallacy: "A joint venture or a franchise is much easier than setting up my own operations because I'll have a partner on the ground to do a lot of the work for me."

I look at forming a joint venture or setting up an international franchise as if I were deciding to marry, but often companies jump into a joint venture without looking at all their options. Instead of being smart and doing their due diligence, they jump into a partnership, which in the United States may or may not be easy to dissolve. In Asia, though, it will be a difficult process and more than likely all beneficial claims in the breakup will go to the local company, potentially including the intellectual property.

The most important part of forming a joint venture is spelling things out ahead of time. In this way, it's different than a marriage because in a marriage you will both (hopefully) understand that you're working toward a common goal. However, in a joint venture the partners may not have a common goal. One may desire world domination or local growth; the other may be satisfied with building something that the owner can live off nicely and eventually sell to travel the world. It's also important to understand that your partner has a reason for being in a joint venture relationship with you. You need to make sure your partner's interests align with yours. For example, do you intend to start with them in Taiwan and move through the rest of Asia? If you do, are those also your partner's intentions? Or, is your partner content with conquering Taiwan?

- *The takeaway:* Understanding the interests of both parties, now and in the future, as well as what each party is bringing to the table is essential to understanding the partnership.

However, it's important to understand the give-and-take advantages to in-country joint ventures looking at a Chinese medical device joint venture you may end up reducing margins and selling for a lower price because you have a local product versus a foreign product. Instead, maybe you should look to the Chinese partner to be a reseller (a reseller is typically a company that is a middleman between a company that produces a product and the purchaser) of an American or European product. Eventually, they may grow into an exclusive reseller, but typically it's not recommended to give some exclusive rights to a large territory until they prove their value to your partnership.

The sales channel model of a reseller, as opposed to a joint venture, is a great practice of reviewing why or why not you might joint venture with a company. Obviously, you are choosing a company with knowledge of your market, so they may have competing products and so, even if they agree to be a reseller, which products are they really pushing? We often target companies that are selling to the same clients but do not sell the same products. But in certain cases, like the medical industry, this doesn't play out the same way every time.

Oftentimes, there are different purchasing agents and decision makers for a hospital, so even if you both sell to hospitals you may not both sell to the same people. It is not to say that even this relationship cannot work, but the question is, will it? Perhaps it will work better as a joint venture with this potential reseller than it would as a reseller. You establish some control on the relationship, often not majority control, though; if you're looking to sell to the government (it is uncommon for a truly foreign entity to gain government contracts, although not impossible). Another business structure, very popular in the technology field or the automotive sector is the original equipment manufacturer (OEM), where you manufacture the product for a client who then puts their logo on the product. This has worked very well for numerous companies for years but can also leave you easily replaced because only the purchaser really knows you exist. The end user only knows they're buying the product with a particular stamp on it. Likewise, if your client has issues in other places, your OEM relationship may get devalued without any fault on your part.

The point of reviewing relationships like a joint venture or a franchise is to figure out if keeping the joint venture or franchise relationship is the best option for you or if there aren't better ways for structuring your business. Understanding your other options, and making sure you understand their potential pitfalls, is your best avenue toward making the smart decision.

A small company I recently worked with was interested in taking their products into China and felt they'd found a good joint venture partner, who was willing to bring capital to the table in addition to relationships. The small company saw this as an opportunity to grow their business in China but also as a way to use that capital in their home markets (in this case, Australia and the United States). The partner thought that this capital would stay in China and be used exclusively to grow the joint venture. It took a surprisingly long time for the parties to get to an understanding of their individual interests, even though it was completely obvious to those of us on the outside.

Before entering into a joint venture, you should also ask yourself if a different relationship isn't better for your business. Perhaps your potential joint venture partner should actually be your client, or maybe the potential partner might be the exclusive supplier of your products in a specific area, which would allow you to grow in other areas or sell different products.

Many of the same questions and issues arise in a franchise relationship as in a joint venture partnership. In fact, the franchise relationship is almost a joint venture; it's a joint venture in which you supply intellectual property, and they run the operation, paying you a percentage of sales. Build-a-Bear is a company that owns their operations in the United States and in the United Kingdom, but franchises in all other foreign markets. The first thing they look for in a franchisee is cultural fit next they want someone who has previous experience with a franchise relationship. I've mentioned the single-child policy in China several times. The dynamic of having four grandparents and two parents means that attention and gifts are showered upon the child. And when you consider the fact that China is starved for entertainment and most living quarters are small, which means there's no room for large items, the result is a perfect confluence of elements for a company like Build-a-Bear. But without a strong cultural fit you get variations from a franchisee and more than likely eventual failure.

Likewise, without previous franchising experience, the franchisee often misunderstands the relationship, and either overassumes or underassumes the amount of support and control of the operations you have. Build-a-Bear needs a cultural fit, but they also do not want to teach a franchisee how to run a franchise. This may sound easy enough to find, especially in economies that make up 60 percent of the world's population, but consider this: China's population is roughly 1.4 billion; yet in an active search by over the last three-plus years, Build-a-Bear has yet to identify the right candidate. So, while Build-a-Bear obviously recognizes the opportunities China presents, they will not take on the risk entailed in doing things the wrong way. This story illustrates the importance of selecting the right partners, but it's something that is often overlooked by companies seeking both franchising and joint venture operations.

- *The takeaway:* Don't underestimate the importance of always asking questions and gathering information. For the day your joint venture or franchise dissolves, either intentionally or unintentionally, you need to be ready to run your own operations, or, in the case of a franchise, have a new franchisee. You shouldn't have to learn twice what you could have learned the first time.

Once you've set up a joint venture or franchise, your work doesn't end. Make sure you pay attention to the partnership, both for the sake of its current operations as well as its future operations. Many people worry that their joint venture partner in Asia will steal from them if they don't pay close attention to it; my experience tells me this was perhaps more common in the past (or when you have just randomly accepted or selected a joint venture partner). With a truly well-vetted partner this isn't very likely, but what is likely is that when your joint venture dissolves, if you have not paid enough attention, you'll cede the market to your former partner.

Five Common Mistakes and Myths in Joint Ventures and Franchises

1. *Believing the Only Way in Do Business in Asia Is with an Asian Partner*
There are certain sectors in which this is true, such as certain medical specialties and defense companies; but it's not true in all sectors. There are certain countries in Asia where having

an Asian partner does make life easier; for years, a joint venture in China was nearly the only way to go when operating in the medical sector, for example. In fact, several recent reports indicate that joint ventures in China aren't just unnecessary, but have failure rates of 80 to 90 percent. At least in China, you may need an Asian partner to fail, but most times you do not need one to succeed. There are times when it makes sense to have an Asian partner, for example, if speed to market is important to you.

2. *Thinking a Joint Venture or Franchise Relationship Gives You Better Access*

Again, sometimes this is true. For example, in China today there's a growing trend toward more and more private medical practices. As a foreign firm entering the market, you may find an immediate opportunity on your own to sell to the private medical practices. But with 20,000 clinics and hospitals throughout China, you probably also want access to the public medical practices. A joint venture may in fact give you better access to these public hospitals and clinics.

3. *Believing a Joint Venture or Franchise Relationship Protects You from Legal Liability*

This isn't at all true. The Foreign Corrupt Practices Act will hold you as liable as your partner for any transgressions performed by you or your partners. If there's no better reason than prison time and fines, you need to be extremely careful when selecting a partner in a foreign country. When exploring joint venture partners it is extremely important to vet them, not only for their potential to grow your market and help in building an organization, but also their moral and ethical compass and any past illegal actions.

China has really cracked down on corruption, making this much less of an issue than it was at one time. That said there are still many markets in Asia where corruption is still prevalent. A friend who had recently travelled to Myanmar told me that corruption there was so prevalent that even as he entered the country and they were checking his passport, they outright asked for a bribe. In China, historically, corruption was not so blatant; it was called a marketing expense or offered at two different prices (one in cash, one if paid by check with a receipt issued).

4.   *Not Determining Beforehand Why a Potential Partner Wants a Joint Venture Relationship*

We often assume that our potential partner wants access to our products and intellectual property and so they agree to a joint venture relationship. While this may be true, in Asia, there typically are larger, underlying motivations. It has been my experience that access to new relationships and showing their clout, typically to the government, are the largest motivating factors leading them to form a joint venture. I have witnessed businesspeople in Asia who have done very well for themselves—primarily due to the exponential growth experienced across Asia during the past couple decades—grow lethargic as owner of their businesses. That lethargy then trickles down to their employee's growth interests. As growth slows down, you need to learn how to execute and have superior products so that you maintain market dominance. In addition, building stronger relationships with your joint venture partners by showing how desirable they are to outsiders can help their long-term sustainability by renewing market focus and exploring new growth.

The other reason Chinese businesspeople form joint ventures is because their own product lines are failing. You need to decide if you want to form a relationship with someone who is no longer successful. For example, a large commercial trucking company in Inner Mongolia that was seeing a quickly diminishing return on their product line felt their large manufacturing operations would be perfect for a joint venture with a recreational vehicle company from the United States. In theory, this made sense. They had the land, operations, and experience, and, based upon certain pushes in Asia, recreational vehicles are thought to have a large future potential. However, upon further investigation, it became obvious how much they needed this joint venture in order to continue their future operations. As desperation sets in, you have to question whether a company like this is the best joint venture partner.

5.   Believing the Cultural Fit Is "Close Enough"

The Build-a-Bear hunt for a franchisee quickly illustrates that cultural fit needs to be spot on—precisely, exactly right. In fact, Build-a-Bear has come to this formula through both successes and failures in other markets. Many times we learn the most from our failures, not our successes.

Franchising and joint venture cultures do not work for many different reasons; among them: spurious market, growth and support expectations, as well as different understandings of the supply chain and, most important, the franchiser/franchisee relationship. These same elements hold true for joint ventures as well; parties have different concepts of quality, where the items will come from, how big the market is, and so on. However, agreement on these issues—quality, supply chain, growth, market size, and support expectations—will not matter if there's a lack of cultural fit.

One of my professors from the Executive MBA program at Washington University in Saint Louis, Dr. Anjan Thakor, wrote *The Four Colors of Business Growth* in which he spoke of four different types of growth in business and how they align to corporate cultures:

- *Yellow Growth Strategy* "is designed to ultimately improve the effectiveness of the organization in reaching customers—old and new—and improving its value creation. But perhaps unlike the other growth strategies, it is all about getting *people* to achieve their *highest* potential."

- *Red Growth Strategy* is focused on execution. "This ability to execute and deliver results can provide the foundation for a cost and quality advantage in the marketplace. And if execution becomes an embedded part of the culture of the organization, then this can be a *sustainable* advantage."

- *Blue Growth Strategy* hardly ever acts alone, but is focused around mergers and acquisitions. From these mergers and acquisitions a company must be skilled and focused upon divestitures, establishing market niche, developing its brand, extending its products and services to new markets, and developing new products and services.

- *Green Growth Strategy* revolves around innovation. This innovation is "not incremental improvements like in the Red quadrant; rather, it's the big jumps, the products and services that break away from the pack. It is about creativity, change, new perspectives and 'creative destruction.' It's about breakthrough new ideas."

Now, review your company to see which category (or categories) it mainly falls into. If you're a "red growth strategy," and partnering with a predominantly "blue growth strategy" company, how does that end? You focus on cutting costs and building quality, while your partner is out seeking acquisitions and adding new companies, making it necessary for you to focus on cost and quality all over again.

At a certain point, you both become frustrated with each other because they want to acquire and you want to improve your current line of products. One strategy has to take the lead, but being partners from two different parts of the world with different backgrounds makes this extremely hard. Perhaps in a perfect world, your partner goes out and acquires and you go in and improve, but more than likely at a certain point you begin to question your partner's strategy and they begin to question yours.

- *The takeaway:* Making sure your cultures align is of the utmost importance.

Perhaps I seem a little down on joint ventures and franchises. In fact, I am actually very much in favor of them, in certain cases, based upon the industry and the business. Where I lose faith in the joint venture and franchise relationship is when people do not come into the relationship with their eyes open and simply think it'll be an easier and cheaper way to go. There are many great opportunities out there when a joint venture or franchise makes perfect sense, and I've touched on a few of these instances.

If you're considering a joint venture or franchise, make sure the decision-making process comes in the planning stages of your business operations and not as a part of the strategy. Figure out where you need to go; a joint venture may be an answer to how to get there; it isn't an overarching design. You also need to make sure that your decision doesn't come too late in the process. Occasionally, companies settle for a joint venture or franchise when they fail to get initial traction. We have discussed reevaluating your plan as time goes on and perhaps a joint venture or franchise is a good change, but by making it a part of your planning process, the decision will be made based on a thoughtful, drawn-out plan as opposed to a knee-jerk reaction.

CHAPTER 11

An Asian Strategy for Small Businesses

Small business is the backbone of society, yet many opportunities elude small businesses because they do not have the experience or wherewithal to evaluate all of their opportunities. Sometimes businesses miss out on their best chances in business because they stick to what they know best.

Small businesses offer a unique perspective on business growth, especially international business growth. Innovation often happens in the international market because the options afforded to larger companies aren't available to small businesses. A small business can't afford to place extra employees on a project, despite its potential, because they don't have the available manpower so they find different ways to get similar results, thus you have International PEOs or other outsourced services that didn't exist previously. Instead they find innovative ways to do things at less expense and/or in a less time-intensive manner. Sometimes this works gangbusters, and sometimes it's not the right decision and the result is slow or no growth. Another result of the lack of available employees to support growth is that success comes much more slowly to a small business. The inability to move quickly—unless you have a new technology or innovation—is an obvious downside because it's nearly impossible to time markets, and therefore getting to market first, which may make the difference between success and failure, is elusive. Some options for small businesses interested in entering the Asian market include:

- Hiring an outsourced sales team that can lead to on-the-ground growth when sales can support it;

- Forming joint ventures (discussed in chapter 10); and

- Forming long-distance sales relationships.

Since Asian culture, especially Southeast Asian culture, is a culture built on relationships, as you develop your strategy, it is important to remember that relationships must be the driving force. So, if you choose to go with a long-distance sales relationship, make sure you make semiregular trips to Asia to build and grow the relationships necessary to sustain growth.

When I helped Gallagher set up operations in China, we had recently engaged in a new contract with the government that would yield approximately $5 million in the first two years. At the time, Gallagher was an $11 million a year company, so this was a large job. Our contracts were with the Chinese government, so we didn't have to worry about the viability of the client or their ability to pay.

However, one clause in our contract stipulated that we had to open an office in China; seemingly, a small price to pay for such a sizable contract. Two years and $3 million dollars later, we had a fully functioning office (many unexpected issues created an opportunity for me to learn many lessons along the way). It wasn't simply an issue of money, it was also an issue of time; it took nine months to have a fully registered company in Shanghai with a holding company that was set up in Hong Kong. Although this was irritating at the time, I later learned that two years was relatively fast for Asia.

Due to our inexperience in the Chinese market, there were other miscalculations, for example, we hired an accounting firm based upon saving a few dollars instead of hiring a firm that had the proper background. Finding the appropriate mix of U.S. staff to local talent was also part of the process. For any business, these missteps are even more costly if repeated; for a small business, they can demolish your chances of success, so I can't emphasize enough the importance of learning from mistakes.

Five Common Mistakes Small Businesses Make When Entering Asia

For any business, missteps like those I made are even more costly if repeated; for a small business they can be catastrophic. While we managed to survive the mistakes, many businesses do not.

1. *Underestimating the Cost of New Market Growth*
Some things have changed in China since I set up Gallagher's office there. Capital funding requirements have decreased, and, in many cases, been erased; setup time has been cut down (although it's still not unusual for it to take up to six months), and there are fewer steps to the process of setting up your operations. All of these are great advances, but that doesn't mean it's as easy as in the United States where you can simply go to your secretary of state's website and click a few buttons.

We have to coach our clients all the time to not underestimate their costs and the time involved in setting up and growing a new market. Inevitably, unforeseen costs as well as time delays arise. This is especially prevalent in less established markets where the delays are longer because more is done by hand and less is automated, leaving room for more errors and questions.

For example, in my experience companies interested in growing manufacturing operations in Vietnam or other small countries in Southeast Asia are typically motivated by the option of cheap labor costs. But they don't take into account the downside. While the labor costs are cheap, the business practices in the country differ considerably—for instance, the time associated with getting simple things accomplished. Something as seemingly simple as setting up phone service or getting the landlord to turn the heat on takes much longer than anticipated. Thus, it's not uncommon for Asian offices and manufacturing facilities to operate without heat or air conditioning.

These basic processes take time, especially if you are not in a major city. They can also cost money and impact your operations. Therefore, when clients come to me for advice, I ask questions like these:

- Do you understand the power outages in the country, both how and why they occur?

- When a power outage does occur, how will it affect your business and your operations?

- Does your business need constant electricity or can you operate with just the light of day as long as you have manpower on a project?

These aren't idle questions. This predicament is one of many reasons why most of the more successful businesses in Vietnam are low tech. While this situation is changing almost daily, to assume that full power is a given is foolish.

2. *Believing You Can Leave an Employee to Run an Operation*

This happens in large companies too but can be more devastating to a small business. Under the best of circumstances, if you bring in a top-notch executive to run your operation, they may succeed. But more often than not, if the whole organization, especially the senior team, isn't a part of the implementation of new market growth, you create an island without a bridge. While starting your operations in a new country with one vetted employee may appear to be a good idea, it rarely works. This employee might work hard, be smart, and perhaps even understands the culture, but the truth is, one person can't do it alone and is going to need help and support along the way.

It's vital to have appropriate support staff built into your initial plans; adding staff at a later date isn't as effective. Essentially, the perception of being an "island" becomes reality to your foreign-based staff. It's vital that you prepare your homeland staff and make certain they realize their role in supporting your foreign-based employee(s). If you don't provide regular support, your employee(s) on the other side of the world may feel that "it's me against the world."

As a small company, you probably cannot send a whole team overseas on day one, so build a plan. For example, plan to bring the CEO or president to Asia on a regular basis; if you have a CFO or COO, do the same with them. Plan regular (weekly) calls, by phone, Skype, or other video conferencing services, with your Asia-based staff that include your marketing and public relations team, your operations people, and anyone else who is a necessary component of the project. Make the project a team effort, so that everyone knows what's going on and everyone plays a part. When you succeed, everyone has learned something and can share credit for the part they played in your company's success. Everyone learns along the way, so when it's time to conquer your next market, no one starts from square one. You'll keep all of the support employees engaged with the entire team.

An additional benefit is that if you send someone overseas for two or three years the person won't feel alienated from peers and supervisors. That also means there's less of an assimilation period when the employee returns home. Studies show that 25 to 40 percent of employees leave a company after they return to headquarters from a long-term international assignment. Many of them feel they were overlooked for promotions within the company and that they no longer have the important relationships necessary to progress in their careers.

Building in a matrix structure of working relationships and reporting is common practice in larger organizations. Effectively developed by Procter & Gamble, and improved and re-engineered over the years, many people have mimicked their example, putting their own spin on the structure. This isn't necessarily a common practice among small businesses, especially businesses that operate with a very flat structure, common in today's small businesses. However, this matrix structure can actually provide a lot of benefits that a flat structure cannot; going beyond simple interactions, it also provides separate checks and balances. Most small businesses should, at the very least, take a look at this option and decide if it'll work for them. By doing the review, the small business owner may find certain elements of a matrix structure of working relationships, and reporting can be integrated into his or her business plan.

3.   *Implementing the Strategy with the Wrong Employee(s) and/or the Wrong Employee Balance*

There are so many cases of companies sending over employees without the proper skill sets or who have the wrong personalities. It is easy to do because you assume if someone succeeded in one place, they can succeed in another. Transferring someone because their personality doesn't work in your current office, hoping they'll work successfully in a new environment, isn't a good idea.

Another area where people mistakes sometimes surface is when there's an imbalance between expatriate workers and local workers. After all, you're trying to capitalize on local costs and/or local opportunities, so why not hire local talent? If you choose not to use local talent, what are your reasons? You may be missing opportunities to capitalize on cost savings, and you may also discover that the market doesn't value the skill sets and experience you bring to the market, at least not at the higher prices you want to charge to compensate for the full-scale expatriate office you'd planned.

To find the right balance, first take a look at what needs to be accomplished. Are you a service organization looking to grow sales in a market and support those sales at the same time? If so, you probably need one or two expatriates to help implement this plan, but you may be able to fill out the rest of your team with local talent. Make sure you are taking care of building those sales channels, and using a local team with built-in connections is a great way to do that. Do you need a large-scale expatriate presence to bring in your corporate intelligence that can be imparted and sold in a new economy, perhaps? Knowing precisely how you plan to run your foreign operations will help dictate the breakdown of expatriates to local talent; you may need a little of one and a lot of the other; very rarely is it a 50/50 split.

Figure out your market value and use that to dictate your breakdown. I encourage clients to let sales dictate both their growth and their employee expansion; this means don't scale up with too many employees without knowing what the market supports. If the market is balking at your high prices, which you need to justify a staff composed of all expatriates, you'll have to adjust the mix or the price point won't work. For a small business owner, this may happen as much out of necessity as anything else. The negative side to letting your sales drive your decisions is that you're always reacting and may not be able to keep up with your own growth if your sales team does a good job.

4. *Assuming You Are Not Big Enough for Help*
Just because you're a small business and can't afford to hire Accenture or McKinsey for foreign growth doesn't mean there isn't someone who'd be happy to work with you. Unfortunately, I missed out on large opportunities and potential cost savings by foolishly thinking that I couldn't afford help. If you're big enough to consider growing into a foreign market,

you're big enough to find the proper support. You may have to choose an à la carte menu rather than the chef's table, but you'll significantly advance your market entrance by putting the right people in the right positions.

FDI Strategies has worked with companies doing $2 million in sales annually as well as companies doing $7 billion in sales annually, but our sweet spot is between $50 and $300 million. Occasionally, we've had to tell someone they're not yet large enough to work with us, but that decision is valuable, if the alternative is spreading yourself too thin too early, and putting your company in jeopardy. As your company grows into $10+ million in revenues, depending on your industry and your interests, markets in Asia begin to open up for your growth, and finding the right ways to execute in them becomes key. If you don't have an internal team of experts to handle this, which is common for a small business, finding the right company to work with and assist you through the steps in your growth is also key.

5. *Diving Head First into the Opportunity*

You are a small business and one of the great things about a small business is the ability to move quickly and seize opportunities. This isn't only one of the best things about being a small business; it's also one of the most exciting. Opportunity arises and you seize it; being a small business, everyone plays their role and everyone gets to see the fruits of their labor come to fruition. What could be more exciting and rewarding?

This is great when you are operating in your own market where moving too quickly may come back and bite you, but it generally doesn't come with the repercussions likely to occur in a foreign market. With the laws that are in place in Asia, if you dive too quickly into a joint venture, you may expose yourself up to legal liabilities with your new partner such as an inability to exit without sacrificing ownership of intellectual property. If you dive too quickly into a sales opportunity, without proper analysis of what the market can bear, you may overshoot your market potential by building too quickly. Or, you may set up an office in the wrong city or perhaps even in the wrong country. Or, you may not be maximizing your tax situation, because you don't have the experience or staff to make sure this area of your business has been properly set up.

There has to be a balance between speed and effectiveness when you set up in a foreign market. Finding ways to grow your business and take advantage of your ability to move quickly, your agility, is central to what separates you from some larger competitors. Finding ways to protect your business and to make sure that you're operating efficiently is also essential, and here the larger competitors have the advantage. Balance is key throughout the process. Gathering information and knowledge quickly from outside sources can lead to an excellent opportunity to grow your business without making some of the common mistakes your similarly sized competitors do.

Asian markets offer lots of opportunity for all businesses, both big and small. The major difference is the impact risk has on a small business as compared to a large business. Can your business afford a 100 percent loss on your entrance into a market and still be around to talk about it tomorrow? If a large business loses $5 or $10 million after two years and decides to pull out of the market, it will be disappointing and senior staff will have to answer some unpleasant questions. But, if a small business loses $5 or $10 million, it'll more than likely close its doors. The margin of error is so much smaller; therefore, you must be confident of your potential and make sure the risk is worth the reward. If the alternative is to lose everything, you better make sure you can show immense growth if you enter a market.

The main point I try to address with small businesses is that they must make sure they are ready and that they are seeing their business potential clearly. Seeing a large business succeed in a foreign market, or a competitor succeeding in a foreign market, tends to get as a small business going. After all, a small business exists to disrupt the market, show the big guy how it is done, and change the world along the way. You can't change the world from home and competing on an international scale is the best way to do this. However, that does not happen overnight and can only happen with great planning and proper resources.

CHAPTER 12

Utilizing Resources: Where to Find the Information and Connections You'll Need

If you look within your own organization, you might find a strong finance team or a strong operations team. When you're looking to grow, you wouldn't turn your back on those strong teams within your own organization, so why would you turn your back on strong resources outside of your organization?

I don't mean your financial resources when I talk about utilizing your resources, although these are very important. What I'm talking about here is knowing what resources are available to you for your own growth. For example, have you reached out to your city, state, and federal government offices? Have you reached out to the foreign government offices in the region or country? To an America, this may seem like a strange approach, but if you were Asian, your government would be your first call. In this chapter, I'll be discussing a number of different resources available to you, what they can offer, when you should reach out to them, and how best to utilize their information and resources.

In the United States, we often think back to the story of someone making it on their own, putting the world on their shoulders, and carrying it forward. These are great stories, but they're just that; they're stories. More often than not, the story of someone doing this omits all the people that helped the person along the way. Mark Zuckerberg didn't build Facebook on his own; Bill Gates didn't create all of Microsoft on his own; nor did Steve Jobs create all of Apple on his own. Don't mistake leadership for doing everything on your own. Make sure you know what resources are out there and utilize all the resources at your disposal.

The most common "ask" throughout is for introductions. Getting to know more and more people that have some connection to your market of interest is indispensable to your growth. With that said, here's a list of several resources that are readily available as you look to grow into foreign markets.

City Governments

City governments (outside of a few major metropolitan areas such as New York City; Washington, D.C.; Los Angeles; San Francisco; and Chicago) tend to be more limited in their ability to assist with growth. Oftentimes, there's an Economic Development Commission (EDC) or a local chamber of commerce within a city or metropolitan area that can be of some assistance, but beyond some peripheral relationships such as a sister city or trade partner, these EDCs usually have limited resources and don't have the capacity that the state or federal government may have. Getting them to see beyond their current limited relationships may also be difficult. For example, going to your local EDC and asking for a banking relationship in Vietnam they may say no, as opposed to their saying we don't, but the sister city may be able to provide further information or contacts. Oftentimes, there's no strong bond between the cities and the limited introduction may go no further than that.

But often these are the organizations that care the most about their constituents and can, at the very least, make the introductions you need to organizations and people at the state and federal levels.

> ➤ *The key ask* of city governments should be focused around introductions at the state and federal level, as well as any introductions to businesses currently operating in the market you're considering.

State Governments

I've always enjoyed working with state governments on international opportunities. Full disclosure, the majority of my work has been with the State of Colorado. State governments and, more specifically, the Economic Development arms of the state governments, have a very distinct objective, which is to grow jobs within the state that, in turn, grows tax revenues (not a revelation, I know). For this reason, they can be an extremely useful resource as you explore foreign opportunities. Many states have foreign offices in different parts of Southeast Asia as well as sister states in many countries, which can yield relationships. Additionally, they frequently have area representatives within the state that can be a point of contact.

State governments regularly organize trade delegations, host foreign visitors (another great way to meet potential clients or initiate government relationships in new markets), and cohost educational activities about foreign markets.

> ➤ *The key ask* of your state government should be if there are any delegations going to, or coming from, your area of interest, what events are being held around your area of interest, as well as for introductions.

Federal Government

The United States Commercial Services is a great resource for initial market research at a very low price. Most people do not know that U.S. Commercial Services exists, but they are the "trade promotion arm" of the U.S. Department of Commerce's International Trade Administration (www.trade.gov). They operate out of embassies and consulates in over 100 U.S. cities and more than 75 countries around the world.

The U.S. Commercial Services offers several assistance packages, including trade counseling, business matchmaking, market intelligence, and business diplomacy. Their services, especially when dealing with foreign governments, can be critical, and you should engage them early on if you know foreign governments will be an obstacle. The U.S. Commercial Services also will help in developing trade finance and insurance strategies for your business to help protect your business interests.

The U.S. Commercial Services is a great piece to the puzzle, but it isn't going to do everything for you. It works with companies across the United States, helping them engage in markets around the world; this work obviously keeps them very busy and doesn't allow for long, drawn-out processes with a lot of handholding. You might think of this office as something like the IRS; they verify your taxes are correct; they don't prepare the taxes for you (and if they do, you're in a lot of trouble).

> ➤ *The key ask* with the U.S. Commercial Services is for market intelligence and business introductions in the foreign market. This matchmaking can be great because, as I've said, of the notion in Asian countries of the value the government brings to a relationship.

Accounting Firms

Accounting firms are one of my two favorite resources for relationship building. Even if you work with a small local or regional firm in your area, they more than likely belong to a bigger network, such as DFK International (www.dfk.com). These larger networks allow your small or regional firm to garner knowledge that they may not have in-house, effectively giving them access to specialties that they don't need in their everyday practice. One such benefit is their country access. Of course, if you're a client of one of the Big 4 accounting firms (or some of the other large firms), these services are accessible in-house, which can be a true benefit.

I'm a firm believer that before you do anything major you should speak to your accounting firm and your law firm so that you can understand how changes will affect your organization. If you don't know the implications of what you're doing, you cannot make an informed decision and thus you may not make the best decision. For instance, if the Trans-Pacific Partnership[1] passes, you may be much better off from a tax perspective to set up operations in Singapore, as opposed to Indonesia, despite a much higher wage rate in Singapore. Your accountant should be able to look at issues like this and walk you through the opportunities and the tax implications.

> *The key ask* of accounting firms is for tax implications and introductions, either to their offices abroad or partnerships they may have in your market of interest.

---

[1] It is important to note that at this point in time the Trans-Pacific Partnership has been signed, but has not yet been implemented.

Law Firms

Here comes the other person you should speak to before doing anything in your business—your lawyer. They should be able to give you credible information that can help you make informed decisions about your company's growth. If you use one of the major international law firms, they can even provide potential relationships for you in your new endeavors.

I also find that law firms within your target country can be a great resource. Finding ways to use them for parts of your market entry, such as setting up your company in a new market, may allow you to gain access to their numerous clients. I'd also note that in-country representation tends to be much cheaper than enlisting an international firm, but you need to understand the tradeoffs for that cost savings. A small local firm may provide some great relationships, but do they understand all of the legal implications of what they're doing on your behalf as it relates to your home market?

> ➤ *The key ask* of your local legal counsel is to help you understand the legal implications of working abroad with your specific products or services, including which markets you can sell into. A good law firm will be able to make strong introductions to either their partners in foreign markets or friends that may have gone abroad.

> ➤ *The key ask* of a foreign law firm in your new market, revolves around introductions for sales as well as the other business services you need to operate your business.

World Trade Center

Contrary to popular belief, there isn't one "World Trade Center." There are, in fact, 330 world trade centers around the world that can offer connections to almost any country and region. World trade centers tend to work in conjunction with their local governments and businesses and, thus, have a wide variety of information at their fingertips. For a minimal fee, you can have instant access to information about who in a particular U.S. state is exporting, where they're exporting to, what regulations are in place there, connections to the local world trade center, and more. I also enjoy the many seminars and conferences they sponsor, attended by informative speakers and like-minded individuals, who can help expand your knowledge of an area.

> ➤ *The key ask* of your world trade center is for information and research, as well as introductions to both like-minded individuals in your local market and the world trade center in the Asian market you're interested in.

Foreign Trade Consultants

I may be biased, but I think growth consultants, especially those focused on foreign markets, are essential (at least the good ones are). Their ability to know the difference between a good local law firm or accounting firm and a bad one will not only save you thousands of dollars; it can save you immeasurable hours and frustration. The same can be said of their ability to know how to best utilize local and foreign governments, as well as the proper trade organizations. They can add immense value to the scope of your work.

The work they do not only helps you in building strategy; it also helps you in its execution, which I consider just as critical, if not more so. Having someone with experience in the market who can tell you when to stop and when to go, or how to adjust a product to meet market demands, is extremely important and can be the difference between success and failure.

However, it's important to ensure the person you're dealing with actually has the experience you need. Reviewing their past work, industries in which they've had experience, and other topics before hiring them is crucial, as there are a number of "consultants" out there that have minimal or no actual international experience and are capitalizing on Google searches and social media websites to get them clients.

> ➤ *The key ask* of a foreign trade consultant is similar to what you'd ask if you were hiring this team in-house. They need to be able to deliver on your strategy, plans, and execution. Like everyone else, they need to have the relationships in place to provide opportunities in sales and marketing as well as providing for your supply chain, if that's needed.

International PEO

It's probable that you don't know what a PEO is. A few years ago, neither did I. Simply put, a PEO is a professional employer organization, an outsourced hiring firm; they allow you to hire someone and keep them on their payroll instead of your own payroll, but the employee works directly for you instead of a consulting firm or a short-term hire arrangement. Internationally, they allow you to hire someone in-country (a local or an expatriate) who works for you prior to setting up operations. There are often time restrictions on how long you can use a PEO in a foreign country without setting up operations first. They afford you many luxuries including managing payroll, taxes, and human resources for your in-country people.

Sending over one or two current sales representatives (or hiring in market) to build your sales pipeline and letting that finance your in-country setup and growth can be a great initial step into a foreign country. International PEOs tend to operate in many countries and can help grow a sales team very quickly across many borders without significant upfront capital and setup times. Finding an international PEO in your home market allows you to work with someone locally who can manage the human resources in a foreign market.

> ➢ *The key ask* of international PEOs revolves around speed and efficiency, as well as potential introductions to some of their other clients in the foreign markets you are interested in.

International Trade Councils

They go by several names: chambers of commerce, business councils, institutes, *etc.* There are some great ones and some lacking in quality. These organizations tend to charge little cost to join, but be careful about what you're purchasing. I find their matchmaking services or conferences are great. I also really enjoy events where they bring in foreign dignitaries. Where you may run into an issue is when organizations (these are almost always nonprofits) try to push too many services on you and act like more than they are. Their passport services are very useful, but their market entry strategy services typically are a waste of time. To many of these groups, a market entry strategy is making a few introductions and accompanying you on a trip(s). This is important but not to be mistaken for a strategy.

> • *The key ask* of international trade councils is how frequently they hold events, who attends the events, and what introductions you might need in your foreign market.

Five Common Mistakes Businesses Make When Dealing with Trade Organizations

These groups listed below are great reference points and, when used appropriately, make life significantly easier when your business is going international. When dealing with some of these organizations, once someone gives you a lead, don't stop there; ask, "Who else?" For instance, if you're working with your lawyer or accountant on your growth strategy, ask them who else you should be talking to and working with to improve the process. This question often leads to more referrals to good, strong organizations, not just those that come out on top of a Google search.

1. *Not Understanding What the Organization Can and can't Do*

There is a time and a place to reach out and use each of these organizations. But you can't expect any one of them to do everything for you. The closest you might come to an all-in-one solution is your foreign trade consultant, and even they will need your help and support. At the end of the day, every organization has its pitfalls, and it's important to think of each of these as a supplement and not a solution. Even when I sell a *Strategy, Plan, and Execution* to someone, we supplement our own services with people from inside our client's organization, perhaps an international PEO, international trade councils, governments, and others. Knowing what each of these organizations can and will do for you is necessary to finding solutions to your questions.

2. *Not Knowing Which to Use and When to Use It*

It seems obvious, right? When you need to hire someone in a foreign market, you reach out to an international PEO and hire someone through them. How about which government entity to reach out to? Is it the federal or state government?

Is it the foreign federal or local government? Your accountant or your lawyer? Perhaps it is both, or all of the above. Going with an "all of the above" approach for everything gets both expensive and time consuming. You must know who to speak to and when to speak with an agency in order to get the answers you need so you can move forward efficiently. This not only revolves around which organization, but, when time and efficiency are in play, you need to know which person in the organization is the right one to access. Reaching out to the "top dog" may work well most of the time, but if you reach out to the ambassador in an effort to get an answer from U.S. Commercial Services, you may wait a while to hear back while the message trickles down to the person who can answer your question.

3.   *Thinking Only about Your Own Market*
As private one word in the United States, we typically don't think of reaching out to our government; but in foreign markets, especially in Asia, people work with and through the government every day. By not utilizing the same resources available to other firms in the market, you're actually placing yourself at a disadvantage. Make sure you think not only of how you're accustomed to doing business; instead make sure you're pairing that knowledge with how others in the market do business.

The best example of this occurred when I set up Gallagher & Associates in China. At the time, I knew three or four people in all of China. I started out by going to each of them and asking them to suggest a good lawyer and a good accountant. I walked into a very large HSBC bank branch and met with a random bank representative, set up my banking, and operated in this way for almost the entire setup period. Had I had the knowledge I have today, I would have known to utilize the U.S. Commercial Services, Chinese government relationships, and many others, which would have made my life exponentially easier.

4. *Communicating Poorly with the Organization*
We all make mistakes in the way we communicate with different people and organizations. This is no different. I can recall
my own experience with the U.S. Commercial Services. When
I first contacted them, I used their online resources to reach
out to specific people in Shanghai and Beijing; I inquired
about their Gold Key Services and wanted to learn more. I got
absolutely no response and, for a while, thought nothing more
about the organization. Then, through other contacts, I began
to work with the U.S. Commercial Services in Denver. They
were able to connect me in to foreign markets and assist me
with the information and connections I needed. It wasn't that
the initial contact was intentionally ignored, but with so much
work going on at any one time, the random email sometimes
gets lost. You will need to find the best means of communicating with each organization or individual.

- *The takeaway: As* a consultant, I love it when someone reaches out by email because I can do some quick
  research on them and set up a follow-up phone call for
  more in-depth discovery. The blind phone call is more
  difficult because I'm typically in the midst of several
  other things and have to run through the process of figuring out who I'm dealing with in real time. Obviously,
  with all that has been said about relationships, meeting
  people in person is best. But it's also the most expensive
  and time-consuming manner of finding what you need
  to know and can be like "finding a needle in a haystack"
  at times.

5. *Not Knowing These Organizations Exist*
I think this is perhaps the biggest pitfall all businesses encounter. Think of my story about setting up Gallagher & Associates in China and my ignorance about what was out there to
support me. I made my life so much harder because I didn't
utilize all the contacts available to me. Many of these groups

would have been ecstatic to help me get us set up and operating in China, which would have saved time and money, and perhaps would have improved our operations. Additionally, at times I could have allowed my in-country team to focus more on work and less on running around searching for answers.

At the end of the day, the organizations listed above are there to help, typically for a fee, but still there to help. It's wise to use the help that is available; it'll make your life easier.

CHAPTER 13

What You Should Take Home

If home is where the heart is, it's also where
business is done. Eventually we return home
from our work abroad, and hopefully we're better
prepared for our work than when we left.

Of course, there are many trinkets and bobbles to take home from Asia and some bigger items, too. Don't we all need a life-size terra-cotta warrior or samurai sword? Yes, I'm joking.

What should you take back if you travel to Asia on an expatriate assignment or regularly commute back and forth? You travel there to bring your business acumen and to provide value to your Asian operation. So, do you, or should you, return home with a higher value to your company than when you left?

I've left Asia many times feeling tired, but I also feel that I am a better businessman than when I arrived. I've learned to appreciate different cultures, beliefs, and governments. I've watched and read the news from a different perspective than the one I grew up with in the United States, and have probably learned more about understanding a reporter's bias than I previously understood. I've listened to lawyers tell me why it's better to have a Republican in the White House than a

Democrat because international trade relations improve dramatically. I've seen how a society can move agendas along without a congress holding it up for years on end; I've actually watched as laws go into action after being proposed less than six months earlier. As educational as this has been, it's not exactly what I'm referring to when I ask "What should you take home?"

When I think about my "take homes," I want applications that can be used in my everyday business activities. So, in this final chapter, I won't talk about mistakes or questions, but rather, I'll discuss five things that you can return home with, and apply to, your everyday business in the United States, Canada, or Europe. These rules of thumb may be easier to fully absorb if you have an expatriate assignment in Asia, but they can be learned if you're commuting back and forth—after all, that's how I did it. I'm a firm believer that there's something I can learn every day of my life and everywhere I am, from anybody. I also believe that most people are happier workers if they regularly learn something and improve themselves.

When dealing with different cultures, some business people approach the market with the idea that their intelligence is unparalleled and they're there to teach. This tends to be a transitory technique because it lends itself to a short-term strategy for growth. Not to mention, people quickly tire of the arrogance, which doesn't allow room for either party to learn. This approach tends to be one that has initial success, but quickly sputters out.

Five Things that Make You a Better Employee after Working in Asia

There are a variety of reasons why people leave companies after returning home from an expatriate assignment. They come back with expectations of career advancement that include promotions and raises. After all, this was the primary reason they took the overseas assignment. They may be dismayed and feel unappreciated; they may not receive the job they envisioned upon return. Often former coworkers are no longer with the company. Things changed while they were away; people that worked for them may have surpassed them with promotions; frequently, the new opportunities they expected are just not there.

Here are a few tips to help you avoid these pitfalls:

- Keep in touch better.

- Begin conversations early on about your return.

- Focus on facts that show why you're a better employee than when you left; promotions should be awarded because someone is a better employee than their competition.

- Sell what you have that your competitors don't; that's key.

- Don't sell that you worked abroad and your competition didn't; that's already understood. What needs to be sold is the fact that you have gained valuable experience that makes you a better employee than the people you're competing against.

1. *The Ability to Negotiate*

Negotiation plays a powerful role in Asian society. I think there's a time and a place for it, and perhaps it's overused in Asia, but it's my opinion that we should take a piece of this back to our own countries. I use this regularly in the office; at the same time, I recognize there's a time and place to do it.

I think you'd be hard-pressed to find someone who would say negotiation isn't a part of their life. We negotiate with our bosses on salary, our coworkers on where to eat lunch, our spouses about where to live, and our children, as we try to encourage them to eat their vegetables (this one I still lose, but perhaps it's because I don't set a good example).

My point is we negotiate every day in so many different ways. Who wouldn't want to receive a larger salary, eat at their favorite restaurant, live where they want, and have strong, healthy children? Yet, we often give in and tell ourselves it's not worth the fight. Let's be honest, at some point there's a diminishing return; your negotiation needs to be stronger when your child has 100 peas left to eat, than when there's just one left.

I believe negotiation is an excellent area where mixing two cultures can create the best of both worlds. Look at the lack of negotiation that happens in the United States, yet the opposite occurs in Asia. Where else in the business environment do we not do this, where we don't maximize our possibilities?

2. *The Knowledge that Everything Is Possible if You Plan*

With strong negotiation comes new possibilities. Take Singapore, a small country that possesses no real natural resources, but it's one of the truly great countries. A country that every 10 years or so is almost completely torn down and rebuilt, so that if you were there 10 years ago you probably would not recognize it today. This country maximizes its assets as a shipping capital to reduce income taxes (income taxes in Singapore are a flat 10 percent for everyone and there are almost no deductions or credits) and subsidize the costs of the country.

Singapore sees opportunities and capitalizes on them. For instance, in the recent struggles between China and Hong Kong, Singapore saw an opportunity to come in as the new jumping-off point to Asia and market entry to China. It didn't take long for people to see the value of Singapore's stable political and economic environment. Today, Singapore is one of the top locations for U.S. firms to set up a foreign subsidiary and, as a result, foreign direct investment in Singapore has risen significantly in the last 10 years.

Singapore is a great example of what can happen when proper planning takes place and all opportunities are laid on the table. Back at your home office, you will use this knowledge to think problems through and find ways to create solutions.

> ➤ *The takeaway:* Reaching great heights and growing your business significantly in a short period of time is possible, but to do that you need to think through the issues very clearly in order to maximize your possibilities.

3. *The Ability to Execute a Plan*

We all know execution is necessary to succeed. Those who can't execute die on the vine no matter how great their planning and strategy, no matter how great the product or service. What we don't always get to see is how that execution plays out, or at least we don't see the mechanics of how it plays out. In the United States, we hire an accountant or a lawyer and tell them to take care of whatever it is; we have an assistant take care of everything from filing some documents to arranging our itineraries.

In Asia, it's more do-it-yourself. You can have a good lawyer or accountant hold your hand through the process, but the bank will make you come in with your passport, your legal documents, and whatever else they feel they need to sign the paperwork in person. Your registration process will be brought in to be signed, re-signed, and re-re-signed. Even selecting your company name, Bob Smith Consulting, will requires a convoluted process.

By going through the process, you learn how to execute in an environment that's almost encouraging you to give up and quit. If you can succeed in that environment, that's a great step in the right direction.

How do you bring this home to your office? It's simpler than most think. You've gained these execution skills in Asia because you had to. Keep them going when you return. I often recognized that I was using them when I set up my own company. In Asia, you're forced to learn how to execute or you will fail.

4.   *A New Way to Understand Your Team*

We need to understand our team in the United States. We need to understand if the people working for us are motivated by money or pride in their work, if they want more time to themselves or interaction to get them through the day. Too often in America, we project ourselves onto others, assuming that they must be driven by the same things as we are. That's easy to do when someone has a similar background to yours. It's much harder to do when you are in a foreign culture and need to understand a 25-year-old Chinese woman who is taking over as your staff accountant as she becomes familiar with the working world. On the other hand, there is the 50-year-old Taiwanese man you recently hired as a managing director, but his family remains in Taiwan. Both of these employees are working in Shanghai, but neither of them is from this place.

These are real people I hired when I was in my late twenties or early thirties, commuting back and forth between China and the United States. Obviously, I was not really in a position to project myself onto their situations. Instead, I had to sit back and listen and learn, not just about them, but how to understand them and work within their boundaries. I was forced to do this with all of my employees in Asia. It taught me to do this when I begin to work with someone new in the United States. By working with people from different backgrounds in the United States, sitting back and learning who they are, I'm better able to work with and understand them.

5.   *The Awareness of the Importance of Relationships*

There is perhaps no greater lesson Asian culture teaches us then that relationships are king. There is no substitute for knowing the right people and knowing them in the right way. This applies throughout Asian society, but the fundamental thread that runs throughout it all is that if you have the right relationships with the right people, you can negotiate well, everything becomes possible, execution becomes a little easier, and you'll build a better team.

> ➤ *The takeaway:* We all need to do a better job of knowing those we work with, building a better and stronger relationship with them, and inserting ourselves in their lives.

In sales, knowing and working with the right people, treating them the right way, and getting to have a relationship with them beyond the office helps build a long-term relationship. If you have a good relationship, when a better product comes on the market, or a better price is offered from a competitor, you at least are offered a chance to match it. A good relationship is a source of referrals (someone who knows and trusts you is more likely to give a referral than a random acquaintance). It also helps you develop new leads. I can't tell you how many people send contacts my way just because they know I'm interested in meeting and getting to know people. If you develop a trusting relationship, you may also be told more information than you would otherwise receive.

There are many ways to go and meet people that'll be useful to your career growth; things as simple as joining associations, continued education, or just going out with friends. Sometimes I tell people to figure out where the people they want to meet will be and go there, but I find that the people who are always seeking out people just because they're sincerely interested in them have the most success. The focus on getting to know and befriend others will pay long-term dividends, especially in today's society, where too many people think only about the short term or only about themselves. So, go out and meet people you can and will be interested in. But there is one caveat—be genuine. If you're not genuine, people will see through it, maybe not today, maybe not tomorrow, but one day they'll see through it, and no reputation spreads faster than a bad reputation.

I can't speak to everything that can be learned from working in Asia, but I believe these five are extremely important things to take back to your office. Again, one of the primary concerns of expats, who work abroad and return home, is that their foreign experience is not respected in the way they anticipated, and they feel forgotten. Not quite what they signed up for. So finding a way to bring back a better you and sell that to your home office is very important.

I recently asked a panel of senior people speaking about their expat assignments what they would bring back when they returned home that would justify the high expectations they had before they left. For the most part, there was silence—unusual for downtown Shanghai. From a company's perspective, you need to bring the most value to a position, which means relationships and relevant, recent experience. So, when you work abroad, consider what you are going to bring back. Can you look someone in the eye and say with conviction what you can offer now that prior to your overseas assignment you couldn't?

I hope this book has been helpful, whether you are considering expanding into Asia, have recently started doing business in Asia, or have been doing business there for a while. If you've been doing business in Asia for years, my guess is you've read through certain chapters and said, "Oh yes, I did that, and it's nice to know I'm not alone." If you haven't previously done business in Asia, and are considering it, I hope this book helps you sidestep some land mines. One thing I know for sure is that working in Asia is fun and exciting, but success requires diligence and understanding. Make sure you're prepared before entering the market. It may be that this book made you decide that your business or you aren't ready to enter the Asian markets. That's okay. It's not right for everyone, and learning that before you spend lots of money trying might mean this book was the greatest investment you ever made.